LISTENING OUT LOUD

THE HARPER & ROW SERIES ON THE PROFESSIONS

On Becoming a Novelist by John Gardner

Growing Minds: On Becoming a Teacher by Herbert Kohl

On Becoming a Biologist by John Janovy, Jr.

Keeping Hope Alive: On Becoming a Psychotherapist
by F. Robert Rodman, M.D.

Listening Out Loud

BECOMING A COMPOSER

by Elizabeth Swados

89-1175

1817

HARPER & ROW, PUBLISHERS

New York, Cambridge, Philadelphia, San Francisco, London

Mexico City, São Paulo, Singapore, Sydney

FIRST EDITION

Designer: Ruth Bornschlegel
Copyeditor: Susan Gaustad
Indexer: Maro Riofrancos

Library of Congress Cataloging-in-Publication Data

Swados, Elizabeth.
  Listening out loud.

  Includes index.
  1. Composition (Music) I. Title.
MT40.S98 1988   781.6'1   88-45064
ISBN 0-06-015992-8

88 89 90 91 92 AC/HC 10 9 8 7 6 5 4 3 2 1

This book is dedicated to all the musicians, singers, actors, and actresses who in the past have been and who presently are my partners in making ideas become living music. And to the audiences who listened and cheered us on.

Contents

Acknowledgments

I'd like to thank Linda Crawford and my editor Ted Solotaroff for their considerable skill and for the time they put in helping to shape the character and form of this book. The challenge of describing a nonverbal vocation was made possible by their contributions. Thanks also to Steve Rosenthal and Jeff Waxman for technical synthesizer information; to Bill Castellino for listening to the theater sections; to my New York University classes for asking the questions that provided stimulus for this text; to Charlotte Sheedy, Jerome B. Lurie, Nessa Rapoport, Rita Wallsh, and Peter Matson for guidance and support; and, especially, to the many composers who shared their stories and opinions with me.

LISTENING OUT LOUD

ONE

The Opening

As a small child I lived near a zoo, surrounded by the sounds of animals and birds. Some of these sounds frightened me: the lion's roar, the bleat of a seal, and especially the blaring trumpet of the elephant. When I was five, I began to count the elephant's blasts and the spaces that existed between them, to notice other sounds that entered those spaces, how long they lasted, how frequently they occurred. Discerning a pattern in the zoo voices, organizing a kind of animal symphony in my mind, put me in control of the sounds and made me less frightened. I also got to know the sounds very well in the process. I re-created them as best I could by imitating with my voice while plucking on a clothesline or hitting an empty pot.

Around that time, I began studying classical piano and was required to practice each day. While I pretended I was playing assigned pieces, I began to spend the time improvising. When the practice hour was over, I would remain at the piano to write songs.

Once again I lost myself in sounds. I explored the difference between pounding a furious chord and touching a single note; the blur of the soft pedal, which seemed to ring the notes on forever; and the zip of three notes played as fast as my fingers could go. When I found a pattern I liked, I repeated it. The power of the sounds grew as I came to understand better how I made them. My songs got longer as

1

I added tiny new sections onto each memorized discovery. I didn't, at that time, think about an audience any more than I'd fantasized about applause for my giant zoo orchestra. I'd found a language that was secret, controllable, and my own. My senses woke up; I sweated as if I were doing sports; I felt brave and excited as if I were a heroine at the beginning of a long adventure. At the age of five, I didn't care about the other composers whose music sat on the piano. The idea that anyone might know my sounds would have seemed absurd. No one else had been there. No one heard what I heard. I owned the world.

Over the years I've learned to speak the language of those who experience the world through their eyes, rather than ears. I can pass by a diner on the road and think about Edward Hopper. I'm aware of the formations of geese when they take off. I enjoy sports, dances, and parks and take great pleasure from the walking styles and mannerisms of my fellow human beings. Left to my own devices, however, I hardly see the diner. I hear the crash and clank of the dishes juxtaposed against Bruce Springsteen blaring over a jukebox while a radio sportscaster shouts scores. I laugh at the geese, whose flapping and calls sound like bicycle horns in a Marx Brothers routine. And professors, street characters, friends, and lovers often remain as voices in unwritten operas and songs. I measure their louds and softs, the patterns of their speech and steps. I'm fascinated by how emotions cause pitch to soar, strain, or drop. Perhaps, in this way, I distance myself from the verbal interactions of day-to-day life. I see the potential underscoring each confrontation or attraction. Song cues some to me during crucial decisions. Sound is the medium through which I perceive life. A composer uses sound to try to shape, understand, and express her daily pleasures and her unanswered questions.

The passion for organizing sounds and the desire to own and shape them are characteristic of all composers. And

I think it's likely that most of them experience these drives early in life. An extraordinary relationship to sound and a fanaticism about it are not skills that one makes a conscious decision to develop. They are givens for the composer, to whom an event is a complex opera of sound that he or she desires not to act in or to tell about but to govern as an absolute ruler, wielding instruments, harmonies, rhythms.

Stirred by a sound that originates in the mind or in the outside world, the composer seeks to possess that sound, to capture the experience of it. Let's say, for example, I hear outside my window an old man walking in the street, humming a Yiddish melody in a scratchy voice. Perhaps I can catch the essence of this with a violin, making it somewhat squeaky, the rhythm uneven, the voicing slightly off-key. The sound should have a haunting quality and an uneven absentmindedness.

Perhaps I hear longing in his voice. I imagine a village near an ancestor's town in Latvia. I hear his mother singing him the tune. He sings it thinking of her, of the loss of her, of the loss of that town and that time. He's uncomfortable on the sidewalk, in the heat, lonely, not sick but short of breath. He's not bitter, but he needs an old tune to push the bad thoughts from his head during his daily walk. Has the old man's humming contained all these elements? Probably not. In the process of translating my experience of his sound, I have supplied them. His music becomes mine now.

The art of taking something from instinct and accident and making it permanent is what composing is all about. And when a composer can retain a sound's original freshness and power even while transforming it, she has succeeded.

A talented listener can distinguish my intentions in the Yiddish melody. Such a listener might identify with the emotional background and perhaps even analyze the technical choices that brought about the expression of longing, unevenness, fatigue, and sweetness. A gifted performer would try to fulfill my wishes by finding the exact position of the bow to produce a strong scratchiness; a full stroke to invoke the old melody, a position above the bridge to make breathlessness. But neither the listener nor the performer possesses the need to transform an old man's humming into a repeated, permanent form. The performer needs to play with it. The listener is nourished by some identification with its mood. The composer is propelled to make a moving structure of sounds, whether inspired by a chance encounter or passionate idea. Gifted listeners find satisfaction in reinterpreting the intention of the composition while it's being performed. Performers dig deeply into the composer's ideas and, with their own instincts and intelligence, bring her hidden intentions to the world. A composer, answering to no one, works alone, sorting through sounds, structures, and dreams.

Thus she is able, almost instantaneously, to analyze the fragments, the little cells, within a sound, whether it comes from an instrument, a building being torn down across the street, or a purely internal source. She knows what is percussive about the sound, what is legato, what melodic. She also knows its pitch, its duration, whether it goes up or down, how long it resonates.

Similarly, a composer must have an acute understanding of time. Time in music is literal; it is written out. It gives the music its pulse, its beat. What effect is produced if the beat quickens or slows down? How does one intensify in the midst of a piece? What about hesitations, a syncopation? How long should it take to develop a theme?

In my opera *Lullabye and Goodnight*, I made a duet from the progression of an argument between a tough prostitute and her pimp. She's holding money back and he coaxes, cajoles, abuses, terrorizes. I can't take an hour to make it come to a violent climax as it might in real life. I must condense the progression into a four- or five-minute duet. I begin by having the pimp's voice dominate the dialogue. He carries the downbeats, the heavy accents. He's berating, threatening. The prostitute coyly responds in syncopated leading lines, fitted in between the pimp's accusations. Because my character is a fighter, her responses to the pimp's badgering begin to grow in length as they do in power. I divide the measures more equally. The pimp sings for four measures. The prostitute responds with an equal four measures. Their voices become a battle of syncopated drumbeats. My "cut time" reflects the parrying of the two furious business partners. By the end of the argument, the characters are singing different rhythms at the same time, both filling equal space, working against each other's rhythms as well as gaining momentum by the differences in inflection, consonants, and vowels. In good composing, words and music are treated as joined forces for energetic sound. The mutual hesitations, duplicities, flirtations, exhausted entreaties, and rages have been translated into musical time.

Different composers might use time differently in this situation. A more naturalistic composer may expand the argument to a twenty-minute operatic scene with interventions from street noises and outside characters. A popular songwriter might find a single point of view and rap it in a two-minute talking blues. An avant-garde serial composer might bring scattered phrases related to the argument in and out of a more abstracted, synthesized urban environment. Any composer, however, must deal with the necessity of setting the argument to fixed time, much as a painter must work within a fixed space.

Music is a nonverbal art form that appeals to our emotions rather than to our intellect. To be sure, sounds can be given a mathematical explanation: if an accent is two beats away from another, it produces a certain effect; if three beats separate the notes, the effect will be different, and so on. But that does not really explain our response. Music speaks to the unconscious.

Composers are by nature believers in magical powers. Throughout the history of religion and mythology, sound has been endowed with the power to produce supernatural results. Aladdin conjures the genie and opens the gate by uttering a sound. The mantric word "om" in Indian religion is believed to clear the system of outside energies that disperse concentration and cause dark moods and laziness of the soul. The sound itself is a kind of spiritual vacuum cleaner. Egyptian lore maintains that one can levitate by chanting certain notes while sitting in the middle of a pyramid. The Hopi Indians have chants and songs that cause creatures to come bearing wisdom from the spirits of other worlds. A lion can be stopped from killing, according to jungle mythology, by producing with the voice a sound that speaks in the direct language of the beasts. Sounds have been endowed with the power to heal, to change weather, to afford access to deity.

Early music was prayer. Incantation is at the root of song. The repeated one- or two-note style of Eastern singing now popular in the styles of minimalist and New Age composers has always existed. There are few cultures that don't pray and whose prayer songs don't somehow influence composers. Gregorian chant strives for simplicity and purity of tone. Its quiet ecstasy winds its way into a great deal of early European classical music, where emotion is meant to be expressed with discretion and privacy. In contrast, the davening of Jewish prayer is less contained. The voice of a cantor is often openly tearful or joyous. The love of God is sung out loud with no need for quiet. I trace the pristine, jubilant oratorios of Handel and cantatas of Bach to Gregorian chant, and I can feel the furious rhythms and sweet melodies of my forefathers' shuls behind Gershwin's and Arlen's jazz songs and even Bernstein's Italian /Latin "street music" in *West Side Story*. The child inside every person believes that a prayer might change bad to good. A sweet prayer gives thanks for a happy event. An urgent prayer asks for guidance in an emergency. Every culture mourns its dead in song. Music is a vast archive of the nonverbal wishes that have been passed down from generation to generation.

In the late twentieth century in Western society, composers most likely do not perceive sound as possessing specific magical properties. They do not believe that sounds cause the sun to rise or the harvest to flourish. Their primary motivation is not incantation. But I think that, however conscious or unconscious, it is part of the composer's belief system that music has the power to make things happen. I wrote my oratorio *Jerusalem*, which brings together the sound of Muslims, Jews, Christians, and the many ethnic groups in Israel, because I wanted to hear those voices combined. At the same time, I believed that singing together would create harmony: the magical element that music, and only music, can produce. A composition begins with the composer's need to organize a set of sounds that is building up in the mind and demanding to get out. It is impossible not to feel a bit like a witch doctor when one gains control of this inarticulate world of sound, orders it, and make it actually happen.

Composing, then, is both a worker's craft and a holy expression, and these seemingly contradictory elements reflect certain parts of the composer's nature. A composer is childlike in her dependence on nonverbal impulses that will make her seem immature, possessive, and moody. However, she must also be pragmatic, orderly, and objective. The composer is a construction worker, building something with notes and layers and time, taking care of what Pierre Boulez calls the "plumbing" of music.

The foundation of a musical construction is as simple as the bass line in the Temptations' song "My Girl." Other foundations are the pedal point in a Bach organ piece and the 5/8 sax bass and drum feel in Brubeck's "Take Five." The composer builds freely but carefully on her fundamentals, taking into consideration the weight, texture, and staying power of each instrumental and harmonic choice. Even when I was very young, I learned not to muddy the clarity of my sounds with top-heavy melodies that covered up my rhythms. A passion for harmony can sometimes drown out the melody it's intended to complement. Too many times I'd introduce a song to a group of friends and watch it disappear behind layers of my own ambitious orchestrations.

Knowing how to connect phrases, to take a melodic line to an exact finish, to build an orchestration neatly into a tune, is as "nuts and bolts" as designing the pipes of one's house. The art of composition is dependent on layering, connecting, and designing workable vehicles that can move at different speeds and dynamics. If the construction is in good working order, then the composer has a chance of cutting through the intelligence of the performer and the listener to touch the unconscious, causing fresh, potent feelings. It's rare that a piece of living music simply explodes from an unplanned work. The exceptions happen in improvisational sessions when the players are highly skilled musicians who have learned, one way or another, the mathematical and other strict structures that give them the privilege of freedom.

In the last twenty years, many creative composers have devoted research to electronic waves—the pulse speeds and decays of synthesized sound. Composers all over the world are programming Oberheim, Roland, Yamaha, and other synthesizers to invent sounds, create samples of those sounds, and add them onto the traditional musical vocabulary. The same mathematical obsessiveness can be found in a composer who is working on a percussive wave lower than any timpani. Beethoven, who kept adding instruments and finally voices to his symphonies in order to create the biggest sound his imagination would allow, would have delighted in the synthesizer's ability to take repeated intervals and expand them, not just through variation but also by pure textural experimentation.

Composers are also very connected to rites of passage and the rituals that accompany them. They have a keen sense of event. Music has always been present during ceremonies that celebrate or eulogize. The impulse to commemorate an event, to give it a musical identity, is a strong one. In Japan, for instance, the Noh operas are connected to seasons. The Jewish Torah is read and sung according to the time of year, and composers write works based on its holidays. Bartok took his inspiration from Eastern European feasts and memorials. Bach and Handel connected their writings to the rituals and music of the church. As we move into contemporary music, the link with holidays becomes less obvious, but the reflection of seasons and celebration is just as evident.

Often composers write with someone specifically in mind. During my freshman year at Bennington College, I lost a dear friend in a car accident. When I wrote my first orchestral piece, I wanted not only to dedicate it to her memory but to capture aspects of her for my own pleasure. She was engaged to a Hungarian, loved folk music, had a loud, raucous laugh, and liked to play the violin standing on an orange crate so her music could fly out her open window. I filled my piece with bird and wind sounds, modal riffs, and a laughing chorus. The *Kindertotenlieder* was written by Mahler for the loss of a beloved child. George Crumb's *Ancient Voices of Children* was inspired by the passionate spirit of García Lorca and the special quality of compassion and serenity in the voice of mezzo-soprano Jan De Gaetani.

Because of their possessive and possessed relationship to sound, composers tend to be tyrants. The way they hear sounds is the right one. Their aural vision is absolute. The result of this tendency is frequently a loss of manners. It is common for composers to be notably rude, walking out on one another's concerts, often commenting loudly as they do so. Jealousy and cruelty are not unusual in any of the arts. But in music, wicked tongues and devious behavior are common. It's an antisocial occupation. Much time is spent alone in a room with sounds. Therefore, opinions are typically expressed in grunts, boos, groans, or even more primary ways. Sometimes such reactions are intellectual— "Why did he get a Guggenheim and I didn't?"—but often they are the result of a more primitive feeling. Sounds can by physically offensive. Offensive music can cause a composer to get sick or bring on a fit of rage. My mentor went pale before my eyes after he heard what he thought was "the strains of those phony pop melodies" in one of my early operas.

Composers are clannish and tribal. They're loyal to their schools and don't forgive defection. They love strongly from the beginning; they influence one another, quote one another, feed and house one another. Then, say, an atonal serialist presents a structured melody and he's "finished"; a modernist begins to write lush chord progressions and he's a "dilettante"; a postmodernist writes a song for Linda Ronstadt and his credibility is ruined. Many great teachers demand loyalty to their singular view of what is truly modern music, what is the only true way to move forward.

I do not share this tendency toward monomania. I believe that all schools and labels have their talented and untalented artists, their share of fools and dilettantes. I try to teach that no one style of music "transcends" another, though I don't believe that entirely. I've stormed out of operas and concerts of new music. I am wary of being anyone's artistic guru. There have been years when I couldn't find a redeeming pluck in one single composition chosen for a grant or prize. The question "Why not me?" or "Why not anyone I can respect?" is often overpowering. However, I try to control my fury and encourage my students to be attentive to new voices whether or not they are inspiring. If a composer works hard at her craft and stays true to her sound, she will become less threatened and may even develop a sense of humor about the competition.

It's difficult to stay calm when listening to one's own music being performed. I know a composer who wanted a section of his symphony to be played without any vibrato in the strings. He stood anxiously by the string section, staring at the left hands of the players as if examining each finger for the slightest waver. He made the conductor and concertmaster increasingly irritable and got himself banned from the rehearsals. He wasn't a Hollywood movie version of a mad artist. Symphonic string sections rarely play without vibrato, and this composer knew he was asking for something not only difficult but distasteful to many classically trained musicians. Yet the heart of this composer's vision lay within a straight, strained sound. The slightest compromise would deny him the realization of two years of work.

Let's say you are writing an ode to autumn, and you decide to use a cello, an alto flute, and an oboe because those strike you as providing the right tone colors, although to someone else they might conjure a funeral procession or sprightly Welsh dancing. And perhaps you begin this sound painting with a walk in the leaves; the cello takes that motif, the flute supplies the blowing wind, the oboe is a flock of geese overhead. If the cello player moves faster than the adagio you've designated, you may end up with something more appropriate to a romp than to a thoughtful walk. If the oboe player ignores your pianissimo and begins to play loudly, your geese are suddenly running amock. A flat alto flute can blunt the air of longing that comes with your vision of fall.

The chances of hearing an effective performance of your work improve if you don't regard your players as the slaves who build the composer's monuments. When they are not taken for granted, musicians are among the human race's most admirable members. A composer shows respect for musicians by writing parts that challenge their technical skills and imagination. A good musician will work hard to convey the intention of a passage, if the passage is clearly intended to put his instrument to good use. Certain kinds of routine orchestrations can't be helped—consecutive measures of rests, pages of held notes, repeated patterns, and so forth—but even these easy tasks will be performed with precision if the whole work proves that the composer used the instrument and its player effectively. Musicians share composers' understanding of pure sound and know the *feel* of it as well. Most of them are motivated by a love of music rather than a grandiose dreams of stardom, and are, on the whole, quite selfless in their desire to serve the piece they are playing.

Although composers can be egocentric and narrow-minded, their clannish propensities typically cause them to be loving teachers and protective allies. My friends and I exchange letters, phone calls, telegrams, and mementos; we buy one another drinks at 3:00 A.M. and leave reassuring choruses on one another's tape machines. Because composing is a profession that frequently involves intense difficulties and disappointments, it fosters a caretaking instinct in those who practice it. Ferocious loyalty and a sense of brotherhood (I say this advisedly as there are so few women) are not uncommon.

Only the most self-important composer could possibly believe that what he or she is doing is absolutely new. Composers recognize themselves in one another's music. They know why someone picked a particular key, what someone is doing with a harmony or rhythm. They are not mystified about why something works. The mystery lies in how that composer had the inspiration or good fortune, even genius, to make such a choice. Wonder and awe come when a fellow composer uses the very same intruments—say a bass drum, piccolo, trombone—that we've listened to all our lives, and still manages to make us feel as though we've never heard those sounds before. Composers exult in such a moment as much as parents do when they celebrate their baby's first word.

When rock musicians listen to Stevie Wonder, they're astonished by the way he comes up with yet another winning hook, or by his multifaceted skills in performing, overdubbing, and producing. I've seen composers respond to the progressions in a Brahms chorale or to the rhythms Bartok creates in his piano concertos as if they were watching a gymnast give a ten-point performance in the Olympics.

Just as families do, composers have a sense of a unique, shared language. It is as though we populate a small, obscure country. We speak in many dialects but in the same tongue. While other people may claim to understand us, only a fellow composer can truly catch all the nuances. If I were listening to a song with someone who was not a citizen of this strange country, I might say, "Listen to that. Doesn't it make you feel great?" Whereas if I were listening with a composer, I'd say, "What an incredible place to modulate; listen to how he brings in the bass; I love the part when it jumps into double time." To a classical composer I might say, "Modulating up a third at that moment, and putting in the pizzicato where the sustain was, sets up the expectation of a resolution, but there is none, and we're left hanging and that's true terror." This might sound like algebra to someone who doesn't know music. I've heard poets become rapturous about the placement of a comma or a pronoun. I can understand what they're so excited about, although I don't speak their tongue fluently.

The limitations of a composer's vocabulary, just twelve notes (in Western music), demand that she be meticulous and patient. Transforming the experience of sound into music is painstaking, and a composer must keep at it and keep at it until it exists on paper exactly as it sounds in the mind. The transformation process demands great organizational skills. No composer in the world can simply throw sounds together and expect them to result in music. He or she must gather them together and decide when they walk in, when they walk out, when they sit down, when they get up, when they are loud, when they are soft, when they speak together, when they don't. There is nothing random in this construction work.

What makes the construction vibrant and original and worth caring about is, on the one hand, something of a mystery; on the other hand, it's as simple as going into a market, picking up two tomatoes, and knowing which is fresh and which has gone soft. A fresh sound tastes good to the ear and brings with it a sense of your mind awakening. It makes you feel you're hearing something for the first time, and you want to hear it again.

When someone who is truly beautiful enters a room, you're riveted by his or her presence, whereas your eyes skid off someone making an "entrance," striving to impress, overly madeup, self-conscious. There is no question which is the genuine article. An authentic sound has an honesty and directness that compels attention. Hearing good music is a little like falling in love. You're not sure what hit you, but you suddenly feel shaky and excited and intensely alive. Superficial music may touch a listener in a superficial way, but only fresh, genuine sound truly moves the spirit.

The ability to create such sounds is surely a gift. But a wide variety of opinions exist about who is gifted and who is merely talented. For a young composer to spend time worrying about which she is is a waste of time. It is also a sneaky way of being lazy. Composers may fall silent for a time, or question whether they can withstand the perils of life in the profession, but they do not spend time wondering if they are real composers. Composing is an art form that leaves little room for self-doubt. The sounds themselves are insistent and irrefutable. You must write them as you hear them. You must write them to please yourself. And, most important, you must love the music for itself.

Composers, like all other people, sometimes resort to wishful thinking. All of us would like to hear thousands roaring when the baton falls at the end of the performance of one of our pieces. But I think that composers part with this fantasy rather early on. Someone seeking adulation or superstardom would do best to avoid composing as a way of life. This is particularly true for classical and jazz composers, whose chances of being neglected and misunderstood are the greatest. In this era, in which rock music commands wide attention and programs in concert halls are dominated by homage to the distant past, audiences are in effect warned before hearing new music, as though they were going to be exposed to a dangerous substance. If theatrical composers stray too far from what has been done in the musical theater for the last fifty years, or what has recently proved to be a box office smash, the audience is likely to disappear, and they will be out of work. Certainly today rock songwriters are the most likely to achieve visible success, but the majority of them ought to know that their work will never reach the limelight.

So you must have a love for the sounds you make that is satisfying in itself, because the chances of other people hearing your music are small. And should they hear it, the chances of their liking it are smaller still. And even if they like it, the smallest chance of all is that they will want to hear it again. There is a long tradition in music, whether classical, jazz, or blues, of composers being ignored while they were alive and working, and being lionized when they died or fell silent. To enter this profession with the expectation of being loved and rewarded is folly.

Why, faced with such grim prospects, do composers persevere? Within every composer, however normal his or her exterior, there lives an obsessive. Music is not born of stable, good-natured, well-balanced impulses, and no one can exist in a world of constant sound, have a fanatic relationship to it, and not be slightly mad. These sounds compel the composer to create music, for only music can truly satiate her craving of the spirit. It fills a need that no lover, child, material possession, or religion can satisfy. It is, in a sense, her definition of being alive. For a composer, writing music is more than a form of artistic expression. It is a way of life.

I've always been fascinated by the poets of Russia who survived long periods of political and artistic isolation and still wrote so beautifully. I am particularly moved by the life of Anna Akhmatova, who went from being a famous poet to a political pariah, to "nonentity," to impoverished old woman, to a revered voice of her people. Besides her life's dramatic struggle, I found inspiration in her constant use of the "little things" in her work. She wrote about hems of dresses, flags on holidays, tattered maps. The act of planting flowers became an event for her art. I liked her simple step-by-step way of perceiving.

It is a gift composers can apply to music. There's much to do. Every sound of pitches and rhythms brings new relationships to the ear. There's always a task of documenting and transforming experience through the private language of sounds and dreaming what the outcome will be when the music inside the head comes to life outside. Each note progresses into a pattern or melody, each sound into a set of beats or effects. There's so little time to finish all the technicalities. I know I can get lost in the terrible despair that accompanies being insulted, misunderstood, or passed over. However, I doubt that I or many other composers permanently give in to our bitterness. Too many sounds interrupt even a happy flow of thought. Decisions don't last. Sounds take over and demand immediate attention. We leave the daily life to go to our rooms and capture its reverberations through our music.

TWO

Finding Your Henry

No MATTER HOW GREAT YOUR GIFT, it may not tell you that a timpani can drown out a trombone, or show you how to set a Yamaha Dx7 to bells that move in rapid arpeggios so that they sound like a Balinese gamelan, or guide you to the exact reggae backbeat that will pump your song to the place where it flies. No matter how many books you read, you won't find between their covers how to double a tuba line with a timpani line to make it growl, how to get a funkier sound from a bass by having the player pluck the offbeat with his thumb, how to use the 1–4–5–1 chord progression in G major to make the strings sound like their tonality is derived from a Central American folk song. These secrets of the trade can only be passed on to you by someone who is more experienced.

There is a long tradition of apprenticeship among composers. Miles Davis followed Charlie Parker, left Juilliard, and went to play with him. Eric Fenby apprenticed himself to Frederick Delius, copying down his music note by note when Delius became blind and paralyzed. Stravinsky's mentor was Rimsky-Korsakov. Oscar Hammerstein was an inspiration to Stephen Sondheim. Steve Reich studied Indian ragas with a variety of teachers. Charles Ives and Kurt Weill had close relationships with conductor-composer fathers. Philip Glass studied with Nadia Boulanger. Liszt hung out with Gypsies. Don McLean used to get in his old car and drive miles to visit Huddie Ledbetter to learn the secrets of the twelve-string blues guitar. Huddie Ledbetter collected the coins for Blind Lemon Jefferson as they rode the trains and sang for their fare.

A student connects with a mentor, who passes on things learned from his or her mentor, just as one generation passes down to the next treasured family recipes. A student watches a mentor solve musical problems, deal with the realities of performance, make mistakes. A mentor embodies technical, philosophical, and moral standards that a student assimilates, appropriates, and finally alters or even breaks away from. A mentor exposes a young composer to a combination of esoteric philosophy, technical wizardry, and grubby, menial work, all of which she must understand in order to live and survive as a composer in the real world. The mentor's very being helps a composer form a sense of her own identity. There is no substitute for this kind of learning by example and rapport.

When musical issues arise in the context of a student-mentor relationship, they take on an immediacy that quickly removes them from the abstract realm. And once a student has contact with a true teacher, that mentor, as well as the spirit of the mentor's mentor, and so on back through time, will be reflected in the student's music. This kind of continuity, placing a young composer directly in a line of musical ancestry, is a characteristic of the craft of composing that takes it beyond the rewards and punishments of daily work. You become part of a tradition. Even the most rebellious composers know they carry someone else's music inside. This knowledge is grounded in respect, even reverence.

Most often, at the outset of an apprenticeship, the student is overtaken by a kind of worshipful infatuation. He or she endorses the mentor's musical philosophy, compositions, prejudices, and perhaps even walk and style of dress;

listens and judges through the mentor's ears; accepts his or her opinions on virtually everything, including the student's own music.

To leave an object of worship is terrifying. When a young composer begins to try her own ideas without the familiar guidance of the beloved teacher, she can be censored by the inner voices of the mentor's opinions. When a composer forges her independent voice, she is ultimately breaking away from the traditions that have been so pleasurable to call her own. As in most separations, the pain of loneliness and ostracism must be endured. Willpower and self-confidence must augment the love of sounds and acquired skills. You have to hold your own against those who are older and better recognized. Later on, love and gratitude usually resurface, but separations within the composing clan are often noisy and bitter—and always uncomfortable.

My mentor was Henry Brant, and I began my apprenticeship with him at Bennington. My music then was filled with African, Latin American, and Eastern influences. I wrote a lot of folk and rock tunes, and I wasn't even sure that I wanted to study classical music. I had the feeling that it had nothing to do with the black turtlenecks and radical politics of America in 1969. But something about Henry was compelling. Dark, intense, wild-eyed, possessed by a mission, he zoomed in and out of class, seldom removing his all-weather raincoat, often in baseball cap or visor, always reminding me of the White Rabbit.

The first assignment Henry gave his students was to write a solo for any instrument in the music building. What we wrote he promised to play. Guaranteed performance is irresistible to any composer, and I set out to tour Jennings Hall. For the first time, I saw, inspected, and really listened to every instrument in the building. And I wanted to write for all of them: chimes, vibes, horns, timpani, piano, alto flute, celesta, temple blocks. Each one seemed to offer myriad possibilities. The choice was difficult, but even before I made it, the assignment had done its job by having all these instruments seduce me.

Finally I chose the marimba. I liked the rows of wooden slats and the hollow, distant sound when I struck them with the mallets. It made me think of Africa, the Caribbean, of pounding on the bottoms of aluminum pots and pans. But I knew nothing about writing notes for this strange instrument. I only knew I wanted to write something rhythmic, incorporating rock and roll backbeats, Caribbean melodies, and heavy soul dance. Eventually, I managed to scratch my little marimba solo onto manuscript paper. I took down the range of the instrument in my notebook and plucked the notes on my guitar. I deepened the sound of the strings so the plucking would sound more percussive. I stuck to simple rhythms, quarters and eighths. I was already hearing much more complicated syncopations in my head, but had no idea how to notate them. I decided that my harmonines should be in parallel thirds because that best resembled the sound of the popular calypso band the Eloise Trio. "Zombie Jamboree" (also recorded by Harry Belafonte) had been a longtime inspiration. Once I captured the melodic and rhythmic feel of the piece, I made sure that my notation was clear. Henry Brant had said he was fastidious about music penmanship.

Henry looked over my manuscript, pointed out a smudged note and asked me what it was, then lifted the mallets and began to play. I had had my music performed before but never with such expertise. I was exhilarated. Henry stopped and glared at me.

"You're a murderer," he said through clenched teeth.

I froze, terrified.

"Look," he said to the class. "She's exhausting this poor little piece of music. She's suffocating it."

The class strained forward to see what he was talking about.

"Miss Swados has written this entire solo without rests." He turned to me then, shaking his head. "Music has to *breathe,* just as we do. Let's pretend I'm this poor piece."

He picked up the mallets and played my solo again, holding his breath throughout. His cheeks puffed out, his eyes bulged, he turned a deep shade of purple. And at the end he gasped for breath as though he'd narrowly escaped death.

"Other than that," he said, "it's a fine little piece."

I found this demonstration humiliating, elating, and, most of all, instructive. First compositions are often as telling as first analytic sessions. They carry intimations of all one's musical problems, as well as one's musical strengths. My piece had solid rhythm and a nice melodic sense, it was quite dramatic, but there was no room to breathe, a problem I was to continue to struggle with in my music.

My real apprenticeshp with Henry began a year later. I had continued to write music with strong Eastern and ethnic overtones, music based on ragas and folk music chord changes. (My Eastern, Asian, and African interests came from an early love of gospel music, Ravi Shankar, the Missa Luba, and any form in which music, theater, religion, and politics seemed to join together.) I was studying the south Indian vina and getting credit for it. Aside from the guitar, I had barely a passing acquaintance with other Western instruments. I was increasingly aware of how limited my range was. I knew I needed to study theory.

So one day I chased after Henry and asked him what was the best way to learn more about symphonies.

"Easy," he said. "Write one."

I protested that I could barely read music. I didn't

know in what order to line up the instruments. I didn't even know the instruments and their ranges. I didn't know the form.

"Exactly," Henry said. "You'll have to learn quickly."

He pulled me into a studio and scribbled on the blackboard the traditional seating plan for the orchestra.

"Almost nothing works in this arrangement," he said. "Consider it an antique. In fact, consider it a dangerous, old-fashion religion. Proscenium stages are the products of mediocre imaginations. Arrange your instruments, as you hear them, to cover the whole space that's available. That's just as important as what you write. The rest you can look up in an encyclopedia. And if you finish it by April, I'll get it performed."

It was October. I said I'd try. Henry's bribe challenged and inspired me.

I decided to try to capture the sonorous bell-like quality of the Indian tamboura and Balinese gamelan in my "Overture." I realized that all the strings would have to drone in open fifths and that marimbas, vibraphones, tuned tom-toms, tuned timpanis, and gongs would be used to replace the brass gamelan bowls of Bali and Java as well as the tablas and other drums of India. I studied which Western horns and winds were capable of creating deep, resonant pitches (trombone, bass clarinet, baritone saxophone) and which I might depend on for lighter running lines of fast melody (flute, clarinet, soprano sax, oboe). In between I wanted horns and winds to drone the fifths with the strings. This was a notion I learned from Charles Ives' *Unanswered Question*, where the strings keep a slow, peaceful major triad feel through the whole piece as if they were the anchor for all the other flighty instruments. I'd never heard a peaceful drone so effectively rendered in a classical piece of music.

My piece was a series of voices learning ragas from each other, developing each raga further until bursts of song imitated each other, competed, and instruments were forced to go faster, higher, and to become more complicated and frenzied. I suddenly was forced to write in every key. I'd never known that the French horn was in F, the clarinet in B-flat; I'd never heard about the viola clef or the transposition from treble to bass for a cello part. These skills became necessities. I pored over arrangers' handbooks and asked student musicians to check my work. The rhythms became a nightmare. I'd intended to use syncopations inspired by north Indian tabla playing as well as Balinese gamelan orchestras. Notating such complex syncopations was like figuring out a difficult mathematical equation, and since I was no math wizard, I always came up short on counts in measures.

I was awed by the rhythmic genius of Stravinsky. I sat with friends at Wesleyan University who were in the ethnomusicology department and counted, drummed, clapped, wrote down. The staff paper seemed limiting, but I knew I had to make some attempt to bring together the two disparate influences of my musical voice. With the separate instrumental parts figured out, I didn't have a clue about how to line them up on paper according to the "rules." I bought another book and studied the order of the instruments. I copied page after page of names according to strings, winds, brass, and percussion, and as I did this I began to realize that certain instruments would smother others if I wasn't careful; others would stick out unexpectedly if I didn't understand in what range they would be subdued or bright.

After I'd notated the instrumental "overture" for full chamber orchestra, I began to find that the piece bored me. The composition didn't cross the cultural gap in a daring enough way for my taste. It was too repetitious, unemotional, and pseudomystical. I decided to call upon the Bennington drama department, the madrigal chorus, and several rock singer friends to merge together in my own interpretation of the Balinese *kecak* chorus (this is an ancient ritual, now become a tourist attraction, where a couple of hundred men sit cross-legged, link arms, and chant like laughing monkeys). I loved this chorus because, even at the age of eighteen, I knew I wanted to expand the possibilities of the use of the voice in Western choral music.

I painstakingly notated twelve rhythmic patterns that crossed over and fit together much like the polyrhythmic sound of a Latino drum ensemble. I wrote syllables for each of the vocal parts that would sound like the appropriate percussive instrument—bongo, conga, laughing monkey, rattle, growling bear, etc. Finally, I composed an arhythmic solo using colors, zigzags, arrows for up and down, punctuations, and even little drawings (a tree falling over, a person falling into a lake) as formal notation. I also made up a language for the story so the language itself would dictate hard, soft, staccato, legato, and loud and quiet sounds through its consonants and vowels. This solo led and interrupted the chorus. (The actor who performed it studied with the voice teacher at Bennington, and they used Spike Jones, Luciano Berio, recordings of wild animals, and African storytellers as guides.)

All this work took place between October and late February. Exhausted and nervous, I presented Henry with my rough manuscript.

He took one look at it and handed it back to me.

"You'll have to do it over," he growled. "It's in ink. Didn't I tell you to work in pencil? There's no way to erase anything. We can't have you crossing things out and smudging the ink."

Devastated and baffled by Henry's emphasis on how the music looked, rather than on how it would sound, I spent the next week recopying the entire score in pencil. When I returned it to him, he said, "Now you've got things in the wrong order. What's the piccolo doing under the tuba?

Do you know what would happen if a tuba sat on a piccolo? The piccolo would be crushed. Think of the instruments as beings. You don't whisper and scream at the same time. And when you copy it into ink, do it neatly. A piece sounds exactly the way it looks on the page."

Furious, terrified, hating Henry, I took the manuscript away, rewrote it, and copied it again, *neatly*, in ink. When he saw this version, he said, "Good. Now we'll get it done. And you have to conduct it, so you'll have to learn how."

I traveled out to Henry's nearby farmhouse and stood on the back porch going through the arm motions of 3/4, 4/4, 7/8. He insisted on simplicity, precision, and control. He ridiculed conductors who behaved like models, posing for profiles and gauging camera angles. He had a special string of nasty metaphors for a famous composer/conductor who Henry claimed "sniffed musicians like flowers . . . didn't lead them . . . looked as if he had a wind machine blowing his hair . . . whose downbeats got lost in his tours jetés."

"What you need to know is when to get loud, when to get soft, when to get fast and slow, when to stop, when to start. The musicians will do the job. They love the music and they'll take care of it. You just give them the indications."

This may, temporarily, have taken some of the romance out of conducting, but it was the best way to learn the basics. Henry stressed that a composer must create signals and diagrams that tell the performers exactly what is expected of them. A conductor's cool authority fosters confidence in the orchestra, and they respond with precision. When the orchestra is moving together in a clear technical scheme, interpretations and emotions reverberate through the dynamic changes in the written score. The composer's intentions are realized by attentive, respectful playing. There's nothing dispassionate about being exact. Henry's beliefs about conducting correspond, in part, to Meyerhold's ideas in theater. Meyerhold believed precise physical gestures and visual images brought out emotions buried in the unconscious. (I allude to this because Meyerhold and his student Bertolt Brecht and Brecht's collaborators Dessau, Eisler, and Weill, along with Henry Brant, are major influences on my particular style of musical theater.)

In April 1970, with pounding heart, I conducted an orchestra made up of members of the Bennington College Orchestra and the Vermont Symphony in a performance of my piece. Henry never made it to the performance, which was for him the least important part of the exercise. But he had been at the dress rehearsal and gave me what was for him high praise: "You got it! You did it!"

We continued to work together the next few years. I copied his music from pencil to ink; on scores that he wanted to change, I cut and pasted and Xeroxed the revised versions. I learned a lot about writing music from the many hours I spent at these seemingly menial tasks. Over and over Henry stressed that the music had to be clear, it had to look right on the page, good penmanship was crucial.

He was distressed by how slow I was at writing down music. I didn't like doing it, and I wasn't very good at it. So we struck a compromise; I didn't have to write down some things if I could find a way of communicating to the musicians exactly what I wanted. Henry's finesse as a teacher was evident here. If he had pushed me too far in the orthodox direction, I would have frozen. If he hadn't pushed me far enough, I would have been deprived of a necessary skill.

Henry urged all his students to explore the broadest parameters of musical range, to redefine conventional notions of sound. We played music shuffling down rock quarries, climbing up stairways, standing on rooftops. We tuned and untuned instruments, sang into tuba bells, shouted into piano bassboards. Henry's music combined a kind of mischievous joy with rigorous scientific discipline, and he was obsessed with getting sounds right. One of his most famous pieces was written for an out-of-tune piano. It's demented honky-tonk. That was the way he heard it.

Henry questioned the past, but he also respected it, placing great store in musical tradition and loyalty to fellow composers. He spoke of Charles Ives, Virgil Thomson, and Carl Ruggles as if they were his brothers and their combined music were rich farm soil, full of American virtues worth cultivating.

I also learned from Henry something about the pain of being a composer. His work was often ridiculed, and I saw the toll that took on him. I watched him go through depressions. I watched him swallow his jealousies. I also saw that he was spunky enough to hang on to some of his anger and that his scrappiness invariably reasserted itself. Henry did not view his music as "art" in the esoteric sense, nor as "product" as some in Hollywood or the recording industry would regard it. He believed it was medicine for the spirit and he was a doctor of sound. He believed that without new music, the human spirit would suffer.

Henry's last gift to me was to assign me a vocal part in one of his symphonies that was being played at Carnegie Hall. I stood in the balcony screeching bird sounds in quarter-note triplets, accompanied by a high school marching band playing the rest of humorous wild nature. Down below on the stage, with Henry conducting in tails and baseball cap, was the demoniac civilized world, disguised in tuxedos and black dresses, uttering its symphonic threats. It was thrilling.

The first show of mine done outside college was based on a Spanish play from the 1600s called *La Celestina*, which was performed at La Mama ETC in New York. I was determined to write an Elizabethan score, and write it for the harpsichord, a baroque instrument. When Henry came to New York to a rehearsal, he told me to untune the harpsichord. The score was too "pretty," he said, and there was nothing beautiful about "prettiness," a term he used with scorn. He wanted some quarter tones, some dissonance in my major key folk songs with their predictable chord changes. He also suggested that I tune the guitar like a cello and add a big brass drum. He wanted the music more off balance, closer to how a poor Elizabethan street band would have sounded. When I rejected these suggestions, Henry wasn't happy and he didn't come to the show.

Throughout our association, the two of us clashed over my predilection for melody. Henry believed that beautiful sound did not consist of the kind of sweetness and harmony that pervades, for example, a great Joni Mitchell tune or a Rodgers and Hart ballad. He believed beauty was found in the kind of unruly scraping, creaking, beeping, honking, wailing, and shouting that surround most of us in twentieth-century America. In the beginning, I concurred in his disdain for melody. But I was at heart a folksinger, sneakily edging my way toward Judy Collins, Joan Baez, and Joni Mitchell. As I grew more confident about exercising my musical skills, my natural tendencies began to reassert themselves. Yes, I found beauty in the honking, scraping, and beeping, but I also found it in the music of Tom Rush, Peter Yarrow, George Gershwin, Cole Porter, rock and roll, and folk.

Henry wasn't pleased with this. He scolded me when I began including ballads in my theater music. He once wrote me a note that read: "There is no need to use the English language in a sentimental, understandable way. If you want to lecture, write a book." He showed up less and less at performances of my work. Our separation became complete when, after helping me to get a Guggenheim Fellowship, he decided I should use it to write a piece for the dedication of the new Bennington Arts Center. I had other ideas, mainly for a rock and roll musical based on Michael Herr's *Dispatches,* and we parted on that note of tension.

That our paths ultimately diverged was a healthy stage in the student-mentor relationship, and though there was inevitably some acrimony between us, it in no way negated the strength or value of Henry's legacy to me, or diminished my respect and admiration for him. And much of what he taught me I have since passed on to a protégé of my own, a rock and roller with a gift for rap music and for setting unusual texts.

The first test I set him was designed to determine if he was serious and committed. I warned him that if he wanted to work with me he would have to do some pretty unglamorous tasks. He didn't flinch. For six months I didn't listen to his music. He changed light bulbs in my apartment, picked up packages for me at the post office, ran my class when I couldn't be there. I wanted to make sure that he really cared about the process of writing music and not merely his association with a composer whose works had been performed on Broadway and network television. I didn't interrupt my schedule to have long talks with him and was unimpressed when he told me he was composing for student Shakespeare productions and after-school cabarets. I distrusted this turn he had taken, that is, his need to show me he was like me. I wanted to hear his own musical voice. I was aware that his generation, ten years apart from mine, was reared on the *Fame* or *Flashdance* model of struggling for Recognition, gaining Recognition, and then the screen credits rolling with no follow-through to the story. Therefore, my protégé was more likely to be aiming for a one-shot success or a high-paying slot or an association with a big name than a long musical life. My tactics were meant to slow him down and test his attention span.

One day he presented what I thought was a genuinely honest and brilliant composition. I'd asked him to find an example of what he thought was 1980s musical theater. He brought in an evening of disco music he'd edited together during his night job as a disc jockey at the Saint, a private downtown disco in New York City. He explained how he edited one tempo onto a faster one, how he created counter-rhythms by scratching the needle against a record disc. He talked about how the changes in songs accelerated as midnight came close and the energy in the room reached its peak. I was impressed by his technical skill, his talent for musical suspense and build. Though none of the tunes on his tape were written by him, the hour-long tape he played me was a real composition. He juxtaposed top ten songs in a way that made me feel as if I were hearing them for the first time. His sense of timing and texture was unique. I wanted to dance.

He had discovered that he didn't have to imitate me to please me. What he'd responded to in my music was its energy. He had rhythms and voices other than mine for his own highly charged inner world. From that small assignment, we found a mutual vocabulary, and much like Henry Brant with me, I immediately put him to work creating tapes for parties, programming sequence parts and drum machine patterns for my movie scores, and exploring a rock and roll theatrical ensemble of his own. Once I was sure he was working from an inner drive and not simply a need to be in the action, I became very fond of him and wanted him close by. Not only did I enjoy his humor, but I learned a great deal about the newest bands—their styles, modes, melodies, and politics, or lack thereof.

Two months before he was to graduate from New York University, a director called to ask if I could write the music for a video she was doing. I couldn't, but I suggested that Tony audition. "Just listen to him," I told the director. "If you don't agree that he's the best person available, don't take him." He auditioned and got his first professional job.

When he subsequently asked me to come to his rehearsals or recording sessions, I refused. I knew he had to go through this part of the process alone. I wanted him to be concerned with the work, not with pleasing me.

There are times when a mentor must leave his or her protégé out in the cold, as Henry did by missing the performance of my symphony. A mentor's job is not to hand out endorsements. It is to teach music, to toughen a young composer's musical fiber, and to give him a taste of the resistance he will face in the film studio or foundation office. A young composer is bound to come up against this resistance. Stunning work doesn't guarantee personal security. The sooner a composer experiences this reality, the better.

At the time of Tony's graduation, I was working on a version of *Oedipus* and was scheduled to go to Greece that summer. When a conflict arose for me, I suggested that Tony take my place—create instrumentals and codirect the music of the show. His time had come, and I wasn't afraid to give him a gift (as Henry's Carnegie Hall concert was a gift to me). Part of a mentor's job is to push a protégé toward separation. Keeping him close is only a devious way of making sure he never surpasses you. When Tony returned, there was no more easy work to be found through me.

I look forward to Tony's next show, and I will go to hear it because now it will be his. And I probably will like some but not all of it, as Henry liked some parts of my music but not others. Perhaps I'll be somewhat jealous and competitive. Those are natural feelings as one watches the next generation ascend. But I'll also feel proud. Imitation and subsquent rebellion are part of a young composer's development of his or her musical voice. As a student matures, the same teacher who could do no wrong at the outset of the relationship can come to seem a restrictive, even repugnant force. I remember thinking, at one point, that Henry was all theory and no content. Years later Pete Seeger, with whom

I also worked, seemed suddenly unsophisticated. When I began compose for theater, Joan Baez (whom I'd never met) suddenly seemed to have a "lousy chest voice," as I remember putting it. These judgments signaled that I was preparing to move on. And just as an adolescent's leaving home is often fueled by anger, a student may expect to feel considerable rage when separating from a mentor. It's all right. It's a necessary part of the process.

While in the process of discovering one's own musical identity, it is important to keep certain things in mind. Do not fear imitating your mentor. Let yourself go. The more deeply you fall in love with the work of those people who influence you, the more thoroughly you will become acquainted with the technique and spirit that informs that work. At the same time, don't restrict yourself to other people's notions of what constitutes a good musical education. Resist the idea that only one style of music—classical, rock, jazz, folk—is worth pursuing, an all-too-common misconception in the highly ghettoized world of music. Rigid divisions between musical styles are illuminating historically and instructive with regard to theory and technique, but they also undermine the opportunity for a vibrant musical life. There's no reason, aside from prejudice and outdated ideas of "taste," why a classical musician shouldn't be able to play a good funky, offbeat reggae or a rock musician handle Bach with a certain amount of sensitivity. The young composer should keep his or her ears open to all the musical possibilities, as well as to the sounds and voices of the surrounding world.

Musical identity is shaped by a kind of individual energy and commitment, and these things evolve over time. Other people will be quick to hang labels on you, but try to resist doing so to yourself. Pinning yourself down musically can quickly propel you into the trap of repeating yourself.

Until very recently, composers tended to develop in

ways that reflected their education, economic status, religious background, or ethnic identification. The neighborhoods in which one grew up or the schools one attended helped shape the sounds behind a muscial style, just as a strong family tie might underlie a composer's loyalties and rebellions. Twenty years ago the turnover of fads was a little slower than today, and many musicians with the same "feel" might dominate for several years at a time. Now technology makes all musical experience possible. There's a gluttony of emotional opportunities. Indeed, a sensitive child has little education in distinguishing real aural experience from the fabulously synthetic worlds brought to us by digital sound. Therefore a young composer can, with a flick of a few buttons, become a Rastafarian, an electronics genius at Stanford, a New Age opera composer on PBS, the next Stephen Sondheim, or a writer of religious country blues songs. The difficulty, of course, is finding a coherent approach to music in the midst of all these possibilities.

A mentor helps the novice composer focus. Concentration and discipline are two crucial lessons for any young composer. Bruce Springsteen recently gave tribute to the style and voice of Roy Orbison. Suzanne Vega admires Lou Reed. The Beatles credited Chuck Berry with their first inspiration. Some of the teenage jazz musicians in my new musical, *Swing*, told me my ideas weren't authentic according to Reggie Workman, Ornette Colemen, and Max Roach. Several young classical composers now believe it's acceptable to break away from their atonal styles and dig into the modal, melodic world of folk and dance because of David Del Tredici's work on *Alice in Wonderland*. I have spent a great deal of time recently mooning over Bobby Short's smooth interpretations of Porter, Gershwin, Hart, and Arlen at the Carlyle Room in the Carlyle Hotel. He is my authority on the piano bar, though he's talked to me only once. I seem to be "studying with" Bobby Short for the purpose of my next show.

There are no rules about student mentor relationships, for no two of them are ever quite alike. But there are certain guidelines a young composer seeking a mentor might keep in mind. Look for someone who has a mastery of the practical skills you need to transform the abstract wish for a piece of music into a concrete composition. A fancy talker whose technical facility is weak will not be helpful. Seek someone who is generous about letting you participate, at no matter how lowly a level: setting up equipment, copying music, tuning an instrument. Somone who keeps you an immobile observer is not doing you any favor.

The most helpful mentor is one who has his or her work performed. Hooking up with someone whose music isn't played won't acquaint you with a crucial piece of reality. Strength of character in a mentor is more important than geniality. You needn't necessarily like or even get to know your mentor as a person. You should know what it is you admire in his or her music, and try to restrict your worship to the music itself. If you find that a relationship with a mentor is undermining your self-esteem—and be careful not to confuse this with false pride and defensiveness—examine your conscience and determine the price you are willing to pay. If you have made a mistake in choosing a mentor, recognize that you may have to move on.

There is at the outset of the genuine student-mentor relationship a sense of distance and strictness. Frequently during the relationship, student and mentor can be quite grumpy with each other. The mentor may chew out the student; the student may feel maligned and misunderstood. The mentor's method of teaching may occasionally bewilder or even dismay the student. When I studied Carnatic singing with an Indian teacher, I was already a fairly advanced musician, but all he would let me do for several months was play the scale on a vina over and over again, first slowly, then faster and faster, then slowly again. It took me some time to realize that this was not an exercise to develop my technical facility but, rather, to strengthen my ability to listen. After several months, he thought I had made sufficient progress and gave me a vina of my own.

Whatever the variables in the student-mentor relationship, one certainly is that it will reverberate forever in the student's music. The connection, once established, is never really broken.

One late spring day, Henry and I stood on the Bennington Commons lawn, looking out over the rugged green Vermont countryside.

"Someday," he said, "I'm going to put a calliope on each of those mountaintops, and on a given cue, they'll all play at the same time and Vermont will be flooded with calliope music."

"What will they play?" I asked.

"Anything they want."

Out of the corner of my eye, I watched Henry as he listened to the calliopes in his head. He frowned. Something was wrong.

"Of course, there are some real logistical problems to overcome," he said. "I'd want to make sure they were absolutely together in tempo, and I don't know how I'd do that."

"Hot air balloon?" I suggested. "To be visible you could wear a bright jacket like the ones school crossing guards wear in the rain."

"It won't work," he said. "Too many variables. What if a wind came up? I think the answer is a fleet of jeeps driven by students armed with walkie-talkies."

"Impossible," I said. "All the static. All the talking. It would be a mess."

Henry looked sad and puzzled. "You could build all the

calliopes in the world. You could hire a choir of angels to play them. But if you wanted one on every mountain, *every single mountain*, you couldn't be guaranteed anything but a random, unorchestrated performance. It's a problem that's been troubling me for twenty years. See if you can think of something."

Ten years later a woman contacted me to ask if I would be interested in composing a piece for the Paris airport. She was trying to organize a huge, international rock and roll Superbowl that would be beamed by satellite to New York, Los Angeles, and according to her, London as well. She envisioned several marching bands dancing up and down the airport runways.

"Won't that be dangerous?" I asked.

"We'll film it between flights," she said.

When I rejected the idea, she asked how I felt about putting the marching bands on football fields. This made more sense, I thought, but the thing she'd said that really caught my attention was "satellite."

"Dear Henry," I wrote. "How about video screens on top of monitors run by generators? The calliope players can see the conductor on the video screens, and the conductors can have multiscreens to watch each calliope. The entire performance can be beamed by satellite to any audience you want."

Several months later I received a reply.

"As long as the technology doesn't make performance mechanical, I won't object. Look forward to seeing it. Henry."

Like many performance art pieces, the football field extravaganza never got done. Nor have the calliopes been broadcast from the mountains. However, I managed to compose an opera in ancient Greek in which the characters performed from different pillars of ruins at the Temple of Venus in Baalbek, Lebanon. In May 1987, I had the experience of hearing fifty voices in fourteen colliding languages singing from the four corners of David's Citadel in the Old City for a performance of my oratorio *Jerusalem*. Though many of my other works boast melodic, folk-inspired tunes and I have no guilt about composing rock scores for Hollywood movies, Henry Brant has profoundly affected my manner of listening to and creating music. He is a permanent role model and bonded spirit.

THREE

The Fundamentals

THE FIRST STEP toward effective composing is not to ponder, with delicious pain, the definition of one's musical voice, nor to wallow in the passionate intensity one feels for music, nor to affect the ideal of Neil Young's song "It's better to burn out than fade away." It's a waste to stay out at the all-night bars trading cocaine jokes, proud of your alcoholism, proud of the manic depressives who went before you, alienating friends and lovers, destroying the work of "sellouts" with your savage wit, too strung out to finish a manuscript, too sensitive and abused to ever make the effort to get your music played. None of this has anything to do with learning about music.

Composers describe their private world through the use of sound. Making such a description concrete and detailed requires not just inspiration but certain practical tools and skills. No matter what style of music you write, you need to understand dynamics and speed, the uses of harmony and rhythm. You need to know the range and capabilities of instruments, the possibilities of the human voice, the problems of acoustics. You need to be able to devise a blueprint that communicates to your musicians what it is you want to hear. A young composer who shortcuts this technical training in his rush to play the role of a composer will dry up very fast. I tell my students repeatedly to show me technique, not passion. Learn the technique, communicate cleanly, and the passion, if it is genuine, will come through.

At the outset of a practical musical education, it is crucial to sharpen one's hearing. The most effective way to do that is to study at least one instrument. Be able to hear exactly how to play a rock or jazz tune on a keyboard, how to finger and bow on a violin. Pound away on a set of drums if rhythm excites you. Work with a guitar if you want to write songs in a folk or blues vein. By doing this, you begin to listen to music that comes from some place other than your speakers; you begin to understand, and to hear, the elements on your chosen instrument. It doesn't matter which one or ones. The point is not to concertize, but to study. And whatever your instrument, it is invaluable to have a solid knowledge of the keyboard as well.

I also favor learning to play a percussion instrument. Western classical composers have a tendency to be rather snobbish when it comes to rhythm, and they may give it short shrift. Even if you are going to spend the rest of your life setting the texts of European romantic poets or creating electronic acoustics, you still can benefit from the sonority and energy in the language of drums.

The second key feature of a musical education is analysis. A classical student learns to dissect a piece of music in theory classes, but any composer should find a way of listening that concentrates on specific details and not merely emotional reactions. Let's take, for example, the mechanical structure of Ives' *Unanswered Question*. This piece uses simple but ingenious juxtapositions of strings, winds, and a solo horn. The strings drone continuously in sustained major intervals, with no dramatic changes. The tonality is reminiscent of Gregorian chant; the harmony is like Bach's. The effect is one of a work that's religious, stern, and wise. The smoothness of the strings is broken into by one phrase on the trumpet. The phrase is written so that the second to last note is the highest pitch. The whole line sounds awkward and a bit mournful. The trumpet's sweet but somewhat blaring voice is clearly asking a question and only appears after a long period of sustained strings. There's no dialogue, no provocation. The emptiness of orchestration preceding the trumpet's voice causes the "question" to come out of nowhere. It seems both humorous and lonely.

The sparse voices of the strings and trumpet are then followed by a flurry of winds in fast-moving time. Their harmony is dissonant, and their rhythm is written in spurts and trills as if they were meant to evoke confusion and mania. There's a subtle harmonic relationship between the trumpet and the strings, but the winds are written in a seemingly unrelated fashion. Ives playfully writes chaotic rhythms and dissonances. Flutes, however, when moving quickly don't often sound dangerous, so there is a lightness to the chaos. This evokes an image of confused response. The timing of the flutes' entrances comes close enough to the trumpet's question so that it appears that they are answering the trumpet. Their colliding lines, however, are clearly not a response to the clear, singular trumpet call. Each time the trumpet enters, there is a variation on the theme, making the question more emphatic; each time the flutes' answer is more chaotic.

This kind of structural study of the piece can go on as deeply as the student chooses. She may want to name the harmonies, count the beats, calculate the mathematics of the relationships of intervals. She may decide to trace a historical precedent for the style of the piece or learn about its relationship to other compositions in its time. Whatever way she chooses to analyze music, it must enable her to become an intelligent, focused listener. There are no rules for this kind of study, and the exercise need not be restricted to classical music. The Beatles' "A Day in the Life" or Charlie

Parker's "Dexterity" makes just as interesting a challenge.

Certain experiences are particularly helpful in awakening one's ears—a sound workshop using vocal syllables and simple movements, acting exercises that emphasize ensemble sensitivity, Carnatic Indian or solfège singing lessons, yoga, or choir practice—one or another should be part of any composer's daily regimen. They teach you to listen with your whole being; they make you sensitive to all the factors that go into a good piece of music. Your internal hearing process should grow and focus as your technical knowledge increases. The composer's territory is the hearing portion of the human consciousness, and its cultivation should never be taken for granted.

Having mastered one or more instruments, the young composer must develop an intimate acquaintance with the others. Most obviously, of course, he should know the range of each instrument. What is the range of the bass flute, as opposed to the C flute, the flügelhorn as opposed to the trumpet? What about a bass clarinet, or the new contrabass with an extra key and an extra string? How do different kinds of breathing and embouchure affect the range of the piccolo? These are simple matters, easily learned, but they should not be neglected.

A next step is to broaden the sounds of basic instruments by changing their original shapes or tunings. Harry Partch, for example, built his own orchestra out of brass and pipes. The Chicago Art Ensemble augments its jazz concerts with large metal percussion sculptures. Henry Brant likes to "change the costumes" of his instruments, tuning a guitar like a cello, placing a cymbal over the bell of a horn. He has often encouraged full orchestras to "blare as loud as they can" in order to study the "music of noise" and the acoustical response of a room to the furor.

When you go to a concert, pay close attention to how the instruments are being played. Hearing Stanley Clarke play the stand-up bass will show you how he makes it become a lead melodic instrument rather than backup in a rhythm section. The classical bassist Gary Karr has demonstrated how the same instrument is capable of carrying rich, lyric pieces such as Ernest Bloch's adaptation of Kol Nidre (originally, most composers thought only the cello appropriate for that full solo voice). George Crumb, in his *Ancient Voices of Children*, asks the oboe player to bend the notes and find microtones usually associated with the Mideastern shinai. Recently, Paul Simon combined the vocal bush music of South Africa with rock and roll to create *Graceland*. This is research, as opposed to collecting tricks for creating novelty acts. In Dick Peaslee's odd and lovely incidental music for Peter Brook's *Midsummer Night's Dream*, characters ran their fingers around crystal champagne glasses. The audience heard the magical voices of the fairies. This is quite different from the guy who plays "Old Black Joe" on tuned water glasses in a David Letterman spoof. I think that once a composer knows and respects the conventional limitations of instruments, she should experiment with new ideas. But to choose a sound just because it's different is the kind of quick and arbitrary composing that creates effect but no resonance.

A good performer will tell you what his or her instruments can or can't do and which unusual choices can be accomplished without coming off like a trick. Sitting with a saxophonist, a violinist, or a percussionist will teach you more than any conventional arranger's or orchestrator's manual. If you *know* an instrument can produce an unconventional sound, get together with a good musician and ask him or her to experiment. Players will be glad to accommodate you as long as you are clear about what you want. They respect composers who write for specific instruments with daring and authority.

Another stage of the process is to acquaint yourself with

instruments of other cultures and pay attention to a world filled with objects that make new sounds. I remember the first time I heard Wesleyan University's student gamelan orchestra. I felt as if I'd discovered a new corner of the universe. The brass bowls, gongs, and marimbas played like a ceremony of bells. I was intrigued by the style of conducting, which, unlike the Western air-traffic system of a man waving his arms, was more like the coxswain of a rowing crew shouting out coded commands, rebukes, and cheers. In Amsterdam a couple of years later, I came upon brass bowls being sold in tourist shops as ashtrays. I collected as many as I could afford and used them in the orchestra of the La Mama ETC version of *Elektra*, which I was scoring.

In Ife, Nigeria, they make a drum whose double heads contract and expand according to the amount of pressure applied as one squeezes the drum against the ribs with an arm. This is the Nigerian "talking drum," and at the age of twenty-two, when I first heard it, I couldn't believe my good fortune to discover that there was an instrument whose range so resembled the human voice that beats and patterns actually meant names and words, and whole solos could be translated into complex Yoruba poetry.

The sixties brought us closer to a superficial understanding of Asian music, but even the most astute musicians I knew had only begun to learn the capabilities of the sitar, tabla, and sarod of India, the koto and shakuhachi of Japan, the kin of China, and hundreds of other instruments from Burma, Thailand, West Africa, and Australia. Aside from teaching philosophical and cultural lessons, the introduction of Africa and the East into Western music brings an awareness of microtones as well as different methods of using the body to make sound. For instance, the kin of China is quite similar to the didgeridoo of aborginal Australia. These are large wooden tubes (much like mailing tubes), and the player blows into them the way one blows a trumpet or shofar, except he or she sings simultaneously, imitating "spirits" with a low, unearthly sound.

I've found that my interest in "ethnic" instruments has broadened my musical vocabulary. When I'm deep into composing a musical scene as background for a dramatic idea, I hunger to go beyond the range of existing sounds. Because I've taken the time to study where and how to find new sounds, I don't stay frustrated for long. Synthesizers provide, for some composers, a great deal more than a quick and cheap reproduction of a real sound. If a composer knows basic computer technology and sets out to learn, by mathematics or ear, the functions that change the variables of a sound wave, he or she can invent whole new sounds. With the coming of the concept of the Midi, the Synclavier, and other advanced computer/synthesizers, composers have begun what seem like musical genetic experiments; crossing an oboe with a celeste; combining dry and wet electric basses with an echo to get a log drum; adding a vocal chorus into the sound waves of a cello; creating sequences of drum patterns upon which one can build enormously complex counterrhythms and unexplored melodic tones from percussive instruments.

I sometimes miss (what is to me) the crucial magic of human touch, but Yamaha and Roland have created synthesizers whose samples (fundamental sounds) are recorded by live musicians complete with human error. Even this addition doesn't replace the sweat and vital emotional connections I need for most of the music I compose, but many inventive composers are delighted by the universe of sound created by electronics. It's cheaper than an orchestra, and for the loner, there's so much layering and texturing provided by the multitrack systems, she can create a huge, brand-new orchestra and never consult another person. (One has to wonder what the romantics, like Rachmaninoff or Tchaikovsky, would have done with access to so much volume of sound.)

Of all the instruments available, the human voice is the most personal and varied, and the young composer should study it whether he intends to write for it or not. Most musical instruments were constructed to imitate different human voices. If you write musicals or opera, avoid the time-worn clichés of the consumptive soprano, the chubby, somewhat unhappy contralto in the character role, the smiling tenor, soggy with love and determination, the portly but nonetheless romantic baritone who usually dies or kills someone, the bass who is wise but old and/or ignored because he's of a lower class. Or the equally stereotypical notions that exist in pop music; every scratchy Tina Turner voice means you're a dirty mama, a high voice like Brenda Lee's indicates you're a hip, sexy teenager wanting to be bad, the Sid Vicious sound means you've come out of a mental institution and have survived to talk about it, a low, sexy black voice (or a white imitation of same) implies that you've just kicked heroin, you're still drinking, but nevertheless you're in there singing. Great instruments shouldn't dictate the content of what they sing.

In Western music, the range of what the voice can do is historically narrow. The contemporary composers who have sought to move beyond these limits and to use the voice differently, say, by putting it through harmonizers or subjecting it to computer technology have arrived at another extreme that can also be limiting. Their approach often strips the voice of personality and feeling, and the result, to my ear, can be cold and empty. Neither of these extremes reflects the richness of the sounds of the human race.

In my oratorio *Jerusalem*, Christians, Muslims, and Jews sing in fourteen different languages. I spent months finding singers whose homelands were the same as citizens of the real Old City and whose life-styles and childhoods could produce the kind of natural singing that a tourist would hear in any Mideastern village. I wanted natural voices. I wasn't interested in conventional instruments, which would undercut the atmosphere of prayer, turmoil, and survival I associated with Jerusalem. I didn't want to distance myself stylistically from the real sounds of the peoples I wrote about. So I wove Arabic religious singers with a coloratura soprano, a Yemenite folksinger with Western rock and roll, a Russian Orthodox basso with a rhythm and blues tenor. The effect I worked for was to have the identifiable American singers act as a kind of Greek chorus against the involved, indigenous soloists.

In *Runaways,* a show about troubled kids, I chose the nonprofessional performers as though they were instruments. My "orchestra" included a tough black boy who could hustle his way through anything; a monosyllabic child of sixties parents, rendered numb by relentless freedom; a driven show-biz kid; a Hispanic boy who felt responsible for his family's economic problems; a young black woman, old before her time; a rich smart-ass filled with self-hatred; the guilty child of a manic family who wanted to be all things to all people. These were kids from broken homes, kids who had seen their parents commit crimes, kids worried about their sexuality. Some of these "instruments" had a hard edge and weren't perfect in pitch, nor were the harmonies perfect; but once again, I chose these voices to expand the conventional vocal types of musical theater performance.

Not unexpectedly, the standard criticism of *Runaways* was that the performers didn't have trained voices, that "the score would have been so much more beautiful if you'd used real kid singers." I wanted to reply that it would also have sounded like a million other scores, that each child was a unique instrument, chosen for specific qualities, and because of that the audience heard every word and every tune that they sang, and felt the emotion they were trying to convey.

The nasal reticence of the twelve-year-old girl who sang as a child prostitute showed her outward numbness. She sang a cold, two-note chant about her "legs opening at one minute; closing at seven; it's like a game." If her little girl's voice had shown sweetness, vibrato, and pitch, the performance would have become a mockery. The boy who sang a song about "making planets with his basketball" had a high rhythm and blues falsetto with a couple of vulnerable, humorous cracks. I didn't want the audience to escape into the usual Broadway fantasy that they'd come to hear a diverting entertainment with a couple of heartrending ballads for variety. By moving away from the expected instruments, the audience was forced to listen to the *whole* of *Runaways*. If they didn't like what they heard, they had the right to walk out. Some did. However, if I'd chosen a cast of voices comprised of "Annies" (from the show of the same name), the audience wouldn't have felt anything but the unconscious memory of the Broadway treatment of sweet children's voices (*The Sound of Music, The King and I, The Music Man*), and they would have been moved in a convenient and superficial way. *Runaways* and *Jerusalem* represent two very specific uses of the voice and are meant to evoke rough, complex atmospheres and provoke difficult emotions.

I say this even though I am also in awe of how much the trained, practiced human voice can teach and transport the composer. When Ella Fitzgerald sings scat, she evokes the mood and texture of nearly every instrument in a jazz orchestra. Folksingers and storytellers can sound like animals, a baby crying, a madwoman, or a grumpy old man. A trained voice can imply an intention that's the opposite of the words it's singing. It can, in other words, reflect all different aspects of the human condition just as other instruments do, and it can do that in unusual ways. Sliding downward into a doomful wail is not the only way to convey that life is less than rosy. Laughter needn't be indicated by a series of sixteenth notes. Sounds other than a moan evoke sexiness. Study your fellow animals, human and otherwise, and listen carefully to the pitches and rhythms of their voices. They are among the most valuable instruments at your command. If you take your observations and reactions and translate them into song or recitative, a trained singer will be able to re-create the emotion, coupling passion with beauty and technique.

Because the voice is the essential mode of human communication, it's connected to the feelings, images, and archetypes of the unconscious. Therefore its range is as wide and unique as the creatures who use it. I once participated in a TV debate with a synthesizer programmer. He claimed that within the next decade, any sound could be re-created. I argued that there would never be a way to computerize the human voice. He talked in terms of mathematics, floppy discs, microchips, "attack," "decay," "sustain," and echo chambers. I answered by singing a piece I'd composed for voice called *Bird Lament*. The British poet Ted Hughes had helped me "create" languages out of ancient Sanskrit and Mayan syllables. I set the guttural sounds to a modal chant. In *Bird Lament*, a creature keens because she is half bird, half woman, half on the ground and half in the air, a prisoner of her confusion. To convey this condition, the voice must go from a woman's madness to her transformation into a caged bird who is crying and dreaming of flight. I imagine the synthesizer expert might have been able to find ways to sample (record) bird calls, women's voices, ancient charts, and mad shrieks. He probably could have combined his samples and expanded their parameters to capture the technical range of my vocal score. But I don't believe that his computer can equal the human voice when an emotion is clear, penetrating, and informed by true experience.

Bird Lament is a tribute to an African chant. I heard women singing in Niger when they were praying for their men at sea. The song also uses the vocal style of a Vietnamese lullaby, in which the mother imitates the desolate sound of her crying baby, which she projects to be filled with grief for the death of the father. Combined with these elements was the added subtext of my own fears, since I wrote the song while ill in Africa, feeling disoriented and lonely. There is no way a synthesizer can accommodate these layers of human experience and their multi-influences on the final song. Furthermore, synthesizers are primarily controlled by the touch of the hand, which is clearly different from the breath, throat, and tongue. When the mouth opens to sing, the whole body resonates like a bell with pitch, word, rhythm, and dramatic motivation. A synthesizer, no matter how brilliantly programmed or played, simply can't re-create this unique aspect of human expression.

A composer should be able to sing whatever he is writing. No matter what sort of theme you're composing—atonal, abstract, melodic, a song for the theater, an aria, a ballad, a drum solo—make the sounds first yourself, experience how they feel. Singing a theme is a good way to test its vitality, to gauge whether or not it has impulse and the prospect of evolving in an interesting way. If you can't sing it, it's probably not really part of you. In order to do this, it's helpful to take a few singing lessons to develop your voice at least enough to be able to cover a strong melodic theme.

A good voice teacher helps you to understand your body as an instrument. By feeling the physical sensations connected with range and dynamics, a composer can learn from first-hand experience how the fundamental technical choices in composing can be inspired by reflexes as much as emotions. If you are in touch with the instrument that makes your voice, you will more deeply understand the mechanisms of other instruments and their personalities.

It is common for young composers to become absorbed

in the rhythms, harmonies, and concept of their music and forget about loud and soft, the most elementary, though not necessarily the simplest, thing of all. Everything in music, ultimately, comes back to dynamics, which is really the measuring of presence. You need to learn how loud an instrument can play, how soft its voice can become and still create presence. In time you'll grasp that there are mysteries to dynamics that go beyond simple prescriptions for a certain sound level: forte, double forte, double pianissimo, and so on. When two people are fighting at the top of their lungs in the street late at night, there is an intensity present that causes their voices to contrast against quieter sounds. The special element is intention and goes far beyond mere loudness. When someone speaks very quietly, the listener is drawn in not simply because he or she wants to hear but because there is something compelling in the softness. It's said that when Bertolt Brecht wanted to draw attention in a restaurant, he lowered his conversation to a deliberate whisper, and little by little, other people tried to listen in.

Beyond knowing how to make things loud and soft, the composer must know *when* to use variations in volume. Dynamic choices are subjective, like most other choices you make, but you should be able to say to yourself why you made a certain choice, even if your answer is simply "It seemed to go that way. I couldn't control it." Sounds can carry one to unexpected places, and, providing your senses aren't dulled by self-indulgence or deluded by drugs, there are times when you should trust your instincts and go along.

Every individual has a different dynamic tolerance. Sometimes I'm baffled by another composer's dynamic choices. When I hear a piece that builds and builds, like the gathering lava flow of an erupted volcano, and then suddenly goes quiet, it's nearly always too soon for my taste. I want more. Someone else might want the noise to descend sooner. I think one of the initial primary impulses behind rock and roll, and a much misunderstood one, was to test how loud the music could get, how deeply it could penetrate into the atmosphere, not to annoy people but to see how much noise one could hear, because noise can be beautiful.

Some rock and roll composers of the sixties and early seventies also viewed raw noise as a political statement. The power of the electric guitar became an expression of how loudness itself can shake up personal and social conventions. A storm of sound crashing into a live concert audience was "heard" not just by people's ears but by their whole bodies. Minds vibrated from the thudding beat, bass lines could be felt in the stomach, high lead electric guitar lines went straight to the sinuses. The combining of the physical experience with the aural was the next step for a generation of composers who embraced the multi-media of lights, slides, environments.

This music was an act of rebellion by musicians who were assaulting both middle-class decorum and culture. Rock bands experimented with huge amplifiers, feedback, and the distortion of electrified sound. Jimi Hendrix played a famous ear-splitting variation on "The Star-Spangled Banner" that was a hostile statement against the conventional American sensibility. He also managed to create a piece of music that displayed a virtuoso guitar technique and a use of distortion and "reverb" that was imitated for years after.

This "noise" remains music when it is organized and professional and shows a capacity for humor or rage. There's no question that Jimi Hendrix's "Star-Spangled Banner" has its place in music just as Charles Ives' or Darius Milhaud's pieces do for introducing the "ugliness" of factories and war noise into the orchestras of earlier decades. When the Who smashed guitars and John Cage broke up a violin on stage, they were making statements. However, these acts do not provide a piece of music as such, but rather enact a hostility toward previous musical norms. The event itself is purposely noisy, but not repeatable as a dynamic choice within a musical context. These "events" may be memorable in the history of musical culture, but they are still noise.

Loudness can be extraordinary when it heightens the drama of an event and disturbs the audience by a terrifying or exhilarating build. The samba bands in Brazil work themselves into a rhythm and volume frenzy for purification rituals. Flamenco singers do the same when they go for what Lorca identified as *duende* (the real soul of the music). I love Beethoven's Ninth because one can feel him pulling out every stop, using every instrument, as he heads toward the climax, pushing the volume to its limit, and, when there's nowhere else to go, adding the chorus to take the sound level one step further. Beethoven, of course, is praised for this now, but was denigrated in his time. He was what many of my rock composer friends proudly call a true "head basher." But Beethoven's quest for loudness was rooted in a strictly constructed series of themes, variations, and harmonic and rhythmic builds. There's nothing random in the work, and the listener can feel the composer's religious intensity. This is music, not noise.

A composer who loves intensity, like me, has to be cautious about not getting carried away with it. If it takes precedence over the truth of the sound, the fraudulence will come through. Dynamics still must be born out of the life of the melodies and rhythms. Mindless repetition, which is so popular in some minimalist and rock music, is not a substitute for a good new idea. Henry Brant had to teach me about rests because without silence there is no contrast. Silence should be treated as sound because it is during those essential rests that we absorb overtones of what came before and anticipate the energy of what is coming next.

A matter closely related to dynamics is acoustics. A young composer should be acquainted with all the variables acoustical conditions can cause in the performance of a piece. It is unlikely that you will often have the opportunity of writing for a particular place. But you may well imagine a space—say the opera house in Milan or Paris, the Grand Canyon, the Taj Mahal—and include the appropriate dynamics in your composition, making the imagined space present in the music in the same way that a set on a stage indicates the playwright's intention of place.

The specific acoustics of different settings change even the best-thought-out dynamics. High ceilings do one thing to sound, low ceilings another. If you remain ignorant of the spaces in which your music might be performed, you'll be disappointed by the differences between what is in your head and what you hear live. Unfortunately, at this time in history, American concerts are often performed in the acoustically treated, visually overendowed, pleated-ceilinged, plush-carpeted, pin-lighted coffins that are the modern music hall. Certainly these were not designed to deaden musical intention, but as that is all too frequently the result, it's best to anticipate the problems presented by such a space.

I always find that music that is sharp in intent, precise in orchestration, clean in its pairing of instruments, can survive even a hall with cotton batten walls. But there are certain known factors about different kinds of acoustics and similar known and unknowns about orchestration. I've never understood why a composer, once she knows the place where a piece is to be performed, doesn't alter orchestrations to keep the music alive. Music is, after all, a living form. A composer who is alive and willing to improve every aspect of a piece ought to be on call to revise his or her work for unexpected circumstances.

Large old churches, for instance, have high arched ceilings with echoes that circle and seem to never stop. In such spaces percussion and voices are a bad combination. The downbeat of any drum loses attack, delays in reaching singers, and gives off reverberating overtones that interfere with the harmonies. When my music for the La Mama *Elektra* was performed at the cathedral in Chartres, the timpani, which originally conveyed a subtle, ominous quality, ended up sounding like subway cars. The shakuhachi (flute), however, cut through the space like Elektra's calm, defiant voice. Therefore, I reduced the drumrolls and filled the score with more shakuhachi. Whispers carried like brilliant rattles, while low, loud screams got lost in the walls. The original tempos seemed to slow down in the immense liveness of the glass and stone. I didn't rewrite my score completely; I simply emphasized the clearest voices for that space. Though some of this adaptation is a conductor's job, or a collaboration between composer and conductor, the composer should open himself to being challenged and reinspired by the questions a space requires.

Performing outdoors presents other kinds of problems, the most urgent of which is providing a strong center of focus. An exercise that I recommend to any young composer is getting together with an ensemble of friends and, against all the distractions they can muster, maintaining an exact beat. I went through this experience, a true trial by fire, when I was in Africa and wanted to learn how to play the talking drum. I was invited to a courtyard filled with amused drummers (women do *not* play drums in Nigeria), handed a drum, and told to keep the beat. No problem, I thought, until they began trying to pull me off the pulse. They tried to trick me, to scare me. Someone would come in unexpectedly, someone else would play close to the beat but just slightly slower. They would speed up, slow down, come up from behind and try to kick me forward. I clung desperately to my tiny corridor of space and time, feeling different pulses bumping together, feeling the pull one instrument can exert over another.

I did manage to hang on, but it was a tremendous

struggle. However, once I passed the test, the drummers let up and taught me some phrases. They hadn't tested me to be spiteful or to demonstrate their power. They simply wanted to know if I was up to the task. Ensemble playing has a danger to it. It is a machine of sounds, each one equally important, that can break down at any moment if one player errs. Keeping the beat in an outdoor space, where it's difficult to hear, where babies cry, airplanes buzz, and sound goes off into uncontrollable directions, is crucial.

If you want to write for out-of-doors, or if your piece is being played in the open, in spite of your wishes, check the ensemble's seating plan. It's important that the musicians can see as well as hear each other. Be prepared for Western stringed instruments to disappear in their lower ranges. I always rewrite multipart harmonies for a strong unison line (especially if the space is without walls or a band shell). Percussion, reeds, and certain brass can be relied on. Sometimes a composer simply must reorchestrate on the spot to save a performance. Sometimes sudden reconsideration brings a whole new life to an idea.

Travel, which I'll say more about later, is helpful in a young composer's acoustical education. Hearing music in, for example, the ancient Temple of Venus in Baalbek, the old opera house in Rome, a basement pub in London, or a metro stop in Paris not only gives you a sense of what inspired your musical ancestors but also introduces you to the magic of performance in such places.

Once a composer knows what sounds he or she wants to hear, the next step is to learn how to translate that desire into a blueprint. The concept of the music is yours, but it is musicians who will carry it out. If you cannot communicate the concept clearly to them, the blood, sweat, and tears you expended fashioning it will be virtually wasted. You must develop a vocabulary that will allow you to move from the abstract to the concrete. A blueprint (which may not be a standard score) is a way of making certain that the sounds that exist in your mind can be given life.

There are several ways of communicating with musicians, some of them more common to one form of music than another. But whatever sort of music you intend to write—classical, rock, jazz, theater, film, dance—I think it is important to become acquainted with all the methods available. Each one has its value, and mastering all of them allows you to work with different sorts of musicians. One thing most musicians have in common, however, is an impatience with incompetence and imprecision. Whatever form your blueprint takes, it should be an accurate representation of your specific desires.

The written score, signs and symbols neatly marked on the manuscript paper in black ink, is one kind of blueprint. Since early times, people have sought to indicate on paper the up and down nature of musical lines, the length of time a note was held, and so on, thus assuring that a piece of music could be repeated. Classical notation is partially derived from the chanting of the Torah (and tropes) and the beautiful medieval square notes, some filled in, some not, depending on their value. Gradually, these evolved into the whole, half, and quarter notes that, along with rests and tempo and dynamic designations, comprise the system of musical notation we use today. When you place these symbols on staff paper, you are painting a portrait of the personality of your music. You are describing accurately the stops, starts, key and tempo changes, harmonies, sharps and flats, that you want to hear. Any young composer who wants to write classical music, or a musical, or charts for arranging, or a film score—in short, who wants to have a professional career—should be able to notate or collaborate with someone who does.

Of course, you must understand that even with the best blueprint, you may never hear performed exactly what you hear in your head. And you will never hear a piece played precisely the same way twice. There are too many variables involved in performance: the environment, the temperament and interpretation of the conductor, the skills of the players, the audience listening to the music. Music triggers nonverbal, highly personal responses in its listeners, as well as intellectual and artistic ones. No two people hear something the same way. High sounds and low sounds affect my senses differently from the way they do yours. Harmonies evoke associations from the past that are highly individual. The human ear is an extraordinarily mysterious and complex piece of machinery, as is the mind that responds to its signals. Composers cannot control their audiences' responses to their music, nor many of the other variables. But they can make certain that their intention, at least, is clear.

During the twentieth century, the notation system has been expanded as composers have attempted to indicate atonal impulses with as much accuracy as possible. Luciano Berio, for example, scores quarter tones, the bending of notes, the bending of the vocal line. George Crumb's scores, which are beautiful enough to hang in the Whitney Museum, also depict basic instructions on how instruments and voices are to go beyond the twelve-tone limit, how to execute quarter tones, how to enter at times that are not easily designated. Stravinsky kept within the conventional use of the measure but created unfamiliar rhythms by juxtaposing measures of unexpected beats in midstream. A Philip Glass or Steve Reich score looks similar to ethnomusicologists' attempts to notate African music in which time patterns overlap, work against each other, come together, then diverge again. The electronic language used in synthesizer music, with its emphasis on sound waves, cycles per second of electronic reverberations, and decay time within notes, is another recent addition to notation vocabulary. It reads like code, but many young composers are learning to speak it fluently.

Some composers, however, are unable to deal with any system of notation, and that is nothing to be ashamed of. An inability to write down music won't prevent you from having a full and satisfying musical career if you are schooled in the ways of getting your music to players and the public. A commercial career will require a relationship with arrangers and orchestrators, but if you work by ear, do not be daunted by someone who can read. The history of jazz, blues, and rock and roll makes a substantial case for excellent and original ear-trained musicians. Western music is the music that is most dependent on notation.

Some composers have such capacious and comprehensive ears that they can hear ten, fifteen, twenty parts going on at once and can dictate them orally to the musicians who are to play them. In order to keep the confidence of the players, a composer has to be able to get across complex ideas in an expressive shorthand. For example, the music director of *Rap Mastern Ronnie* insisted on a heavy downbeat, slow tempo, and slinky interpretation of a blues song. I explained to him and the other players that the "kick and snare were hitting too hard, the 'feel' was too seventies rock blues," and I wanted "eighths on the high hat to go more Chicago, urban, acoustic—Rickie Lee Jones." Then I sung a bass line and guitar fill, and showed by scatting a version of the vocal the style of mischief the singers would ultimately take on. Meanwhile, expensive studio time was ticking away. In fifteen minutes we redid the arrangement to my satisfaction.

Most composers who work this way have backgrounds in jazz, rock, or Eastern music, where the oral transmission of melody and rhythm serves as effectively as written notation. A songwriter, for example, may scat out the rhythm track, perhaps telling the drummer to keep a straight

4/4, then sing out lines to the bass and guitar players and to the vocalist and backup singers, who may or may not write down the lines. I don't know of any rock group from the Beatles to the Talking Heads who didn't begin with this composing method. Generally the composer plays most of the instruments and knows what they can do and also can depend on a strong collective understanding among the members of a band or orchestra, and a shared vocabulary that develops over time. The composer, in this instance, is like a theater director, presenting themes and ideas that excite the players, molding the style of the music by sharp metaphors and comparisons.

A composer who works this way is probably more concerned with color, dynamics, energy, and timbre than with controlling every note within a chord change. She finds that a flourish introduced by a fellow musician enhances a moment and accepts the idea gratefully. The composer has instant access to sounds that are not written down, and the freedom to adapt quickly to the needs and opportunities of the moment. Often the music that results has a special vitality and even urgency. In improvisation, you work very specifically with individuals and their interpretations of the music. Thus, when one player leaves the group, the music inevitably changes. In improvisation, the blueprint is in a sense modified by the playing itself. The concept belongs to the composer, but each player makes a large contribution.

In a group that finds its identity through improvisation, there is sometimes no room for set compositions as such. Indeed, the group may believe that its detours are the most interesting thing it does. Perhaps the group is playing in G major, and, acting on an impulse, one player moves into E minor. The group then drifts in that direction, and then, in E minor, the baritone sax player switches to the tenor, changing the feeling, and then the clarinet comes in with a descant, carrying them all to another place, and all this happens because someone meandered, went for a walk, and everyone followed. The duets that Chick Corea and Herbie Hancock do on the piano are filled with this wonderful kind of travel, but only masterful technicians can carry off such risky playing.

Occasionally all methods of making a blueprint are used in the development of a single piece of music. In the theater, for instance, it is not uncommon for a composer to begin with a song or an orchestral idea and to gather some musicians together to improvise on that. As the playing becomes more elaborate, the composer's idea evolves, and he or she may begin to sing lines to the musicians, who write them down. The composer then takes these ideas back and, working with an orchestrator or alone, sets down the music in its final written form.

A classical composer typically uses a written blueprint, a jazz or rock artist typically relies on improvisation. But I think a young composer should be fluent in both notation and improvisation. Why should someone involved in rock miss the opportunity of working with violins and cellos? Think what the Eurythmics could do if they had the facility to score for a hundred instruments. By the same token, a classical composer whose idea of syncopation doesn't go beyond Stravinsky could benefit by calling out chord changes to a tight jazz ensemble or reggae rhythm section.

Being able to communicate your musical intentions ensures that your music, however complex or unconventional, will be performed with authority. Once, in an effort to re-create one of the plagues in the Book of Exodus (the one that laid low the beasts with disease and famine), I combined the sound of voices singing through cardboard mailing tubes with the bowing of the side of a Japanese gong, an overblowing flute, a harmonium, and a lightning fast minor-modal riff squealing on a violin. The tubes, which make the voice crack into harmonics, created the sound of the cattle cries, the gong was the desert wind, the flute supplied the bright, blinding sun or drought, the harmonium and violin evoked the Jewish themes of the story. I told the musicians exactly what I wanted, and I persevered until they got it. Because I was clear, my idea had authority, and the musicians, who knew their bows, mallets, and embouchures, played with equal authority. If you haven't learned how to communicate with the performers, one of two things is likely to happen: the piece will come together in an arbitrary way that has little coherence and drive, or the musicians' strengths will take over at your expense.

I have used different methods of communicating with musicians in the course of my career, but I prefer the way of working that best accords with my fundamental interest in the theatricality of music, particularly its ability to stimulate the imagination and unconscious. I am interested in exploring, musically, how to create a human exchange or an animal exchange; a conversation between two jackhammers that woke me in the morning or a discussion of nuclear war between two crazy street people; the population of Jerusalem or a café in prerevolutionary Leningrad; or the dream of a New Wave western gunslinger. Also, as I've observed, many of my musical feelings and tastes come from other cultures that encourage musicians to speak with their instruments. In Nigeria, the drums speak poetry. A Balinese gamelan talks to the dancers and helps to tell a story. A tune on a Mideastern oud invokes a dance that commemorates a feast or marriage. The Brazilian parade drum has a special role in feasts of devils and angels, the cowbell signals the beats in the raucous samba schools, shakers and rattles speak for the priests in healing ceremonies. The wailing of a New Orleans jazz trumpet or trombone in a funeral cries out for release from life's bonds. In Judaism, my religion, the long singsong chant of the praying embodies cultural history and ancestral suffering as well as reverence and self-examination.

I want musicians performing my music to participate as actively as ritual musicians do in the above examples. When they blow, or hit, or toot, or finger their instruments, I want them to be totally involved. I want them to know what is going on in the music and to comment on it, for I want them to play with an urgency that only comes with full paticipation in the living musical moment. Because of this, I don't write out full parts. I do, however, give very specific directions about the feeling of a line, and about most of the notes that should be in that line.

For example, in the oratorio *Jerusalem*, I want a descant for the flute. I will give the flute player the line, note by note, either written out or sung, and the tempo. I'll also give a dramatic direction: hold yourself above the Muslim actor as he laments his child, pull back on his grief, keep him from going over the edge (which might literally mean minimize the vibrato and give me an almost airy sound). I'll ask the player to play the descant once or twice that way; we'll listen together and figure out how much is too much—when the repetition goes from being eerie to intrusive.

Or let's say the piece is instrumental and I'm using two cellos to depict a marital feud. I might tell them to talk to each other, using sixteenth notes. Cello A should brag, Cello B should imitate and mock a little. I'll give them the notes, either written out or sung. I'll tell A to become increasingly mad as B continues to laugh. I'll tell B to laugh harder the angrier A gets. Getting angrier or laughing harder will change the sense of time, perhaps change the dynamics. I'll tell the players to take the initiative in speeding up or getting louder. Then we will increase the melodic range of the repeated lines as the argument becomes more desperate, while the improvisation increasingly informs the score.

I remember directing a drummer to use his sticks and the sound of the drum to "beat" a child who was dancing directly in front of him. The child responded with jerks and grimaces that were part of this "score." Musicians, if they're the right ones for me, aren't scornful of this sort of directive. They connect with it because they're encouraged to use imagination and the physicality of music in their playing. On the other hand, they don't flounder because I've supplied the specific notes and the specific tempo. I could write out whole parts, casting every musical impulse in stone. But I don't want to do this any more than I would want to lead an actor around the stage, telling him how hard to sit down, when to cross his legs, which leg to drape over the other, and so on.

Over the years I have accumulated a group of musicians who like working in the way I have described. They also play other kinds of music, but when they work with me they expect to take a certain amount of responsibility. In my music the instruments will come in at the same place, and play notes of a similar feel . . . but the intention must be sparked by the actions of the evening. In effect, I give the musicians the power of an arranger because I want them to feel organically connected to the creation of the music.

One reason I find this way of working so effective is that I almost always conduct my music. If I didn't, it would be hard to trust such a system. But when I conduct, I'm like a football coach with a blackboard, mapping out a game plan, diagraming the plays. And the musicians are the players who will execute the game plan. My feeling is that the music will be best served if the players have some leeway for their own special and instinctive moves. By conducting, I can still control the speed, the dynamics, and the intensity of the piece we're playing.

Obviously, this way of working is not for every musician. Those dedicated to classical technique and classical literature are not likely to find the values they look for in music in this way. They will miss the multitude of colors, shades, and symbols they find in traveling through a piece of classical music. They will miss the sense of connection to the printed page. I respect that, and when I work with this sort of musician I write out a regular, arranged part or ask an arranger to do so.

An arranger can be a very effective partner. The arrangements that Jonathan Tunick does for Stephen Sondheim are quite remarkable. They manage to reflect the dark, intelligent quality of Sondheim's melodies and lyrics, without distracting from the human drama onstage. The arrangements bring forth strong solos from unexpected wind, percussion, and string instruments that would hold up on their own as instrumental pieces.

If a composer is clear about her harmonies, rhythms, and musical development, then an arranger can perform much the same service as a group of musicians working by ear. An arranger completes the composer's vision by executing the technical mechanics that a composer may not have the time or facility to do. The composer and arranger discuss which instruments will best augment the themes, and the arranger sets their conclusions down on paper. A composer must give the arranger proper credit and not delude himself into thinking he accomplished his music by himself. The art of composing is abused when themes get farmed out by a composer and the arranger automatically orchestrates and embellishes according to a recognizable "sound" determined either by a producer or the lazy composer. For many composers, a good arranger can be a valuable alter ego, who, in a creative and supportive way, documents the composer's ideas.

The ideal musician for a young composer who writes down music and wants to hear it played exactly as it appears on the manuscript paper is someone who is classically trained and who sight-reads with the same quickness and passion as an improviser taking a solo. This kind of musician picks up not only the literal designations of notes, tempos and harmonies, but also subtleties of shading. A good sight reader can look at any combination of written notes and hear what they will sound like and sense where they are going.

Both great sight-reading and quick improvisation, however, are meaningless if a musician has a bad tone or a muddy rhythm. A note of caution here for all young composers: sometimes you can fall so in love with the idea of having your music played that you don't really listen to the person who's fulfilling your dream. If you've waited five years to have a song performed, you may feel willing to let a flat singer with an impressive bio premiere your composition. But unless you're desperate, you should wait until a quality performer who likes your phrasing and ideas comes along. Don't be taken in by a musician who drops names and boasts about accomplishments; use your ears.

However, a young composer works, it is beneficial to listen to the advice of good musicians. Let's say an oboe player who has been given a low line suggests playing it up an octave to brighten the tone. Unless you are subduing the oboe's voice for some dramatic purpose, pay attention. If a brass player offers you advice on mutes, listen. He's the one who's been using them for years. I have a close friend in Hollywood who plays oboe, English horn, and all the flutes and saxophones, and whenever I record a movie or TV score I ask her to come by and go through all the parts for her instruments to broaden my sense of what each one of them does within its role in the piece.

It's uncomfortable when you walk into a recording studio and ask a guitar player to give you "sparse, rainlike sounds on a G chord," and he says, "Do you want an arpeggio, plucked pizzicato? Which inversion of the G chord? How many rests, and how long do I hold each note?" Equally embarrassing is the rehearsal where you hand out written parts to an orchestra that's been hired to back up a rock performer and say, "Okay, let's accent that backbeat for a reggae feel," and you get literal interpretations of free street dance music that sound like Muzak in sitcom. These mismatches are time-consuming and expensive to all involved; as bad as handing a fully written solo line to a renowned Hispanic cuatro player and finding he can't read a note. If you can't speak the language of your musicians, you're lost.

Furthermore, musicians become defensive when their competency is challenged, and a potentially creative atmosphere can quickly deteriorate to a room thick with hostility, nasty arguments, and passive subversion. Music is, after all, not made by the most mature and stable personalities, but even so, the world of music would be a better place if popular musicians would educate themselves more thoroughly and classical musicians would become less rigid.

There is plenty of room for both kinds of musical visions and objectives, just as different composers lay claim to different sectors of the aural world. Mozart, Beethoven, Stevie Wonder, Stephen Sondheim, Cole Porter, Steve Reich, Cecil Taylor, Babbitt, Ruggles, Penderecki, Ives: each has a different appeal; each represents a different notion of what kind of sound is beautiful or moving or significant. As a young composer, you will eventually decide in what part of the mansion of musical experience you will reside, a matter I'll discuss in the next chapter. But whatever your choice, in order to be generous and practical (and the two go together), and not simply indulgent and mad, you must develop a vocabulary and be able to use it fluently.

I mentioned that I very often conduct my own music, and I think that is best in most instances. But if it can be painful to be at the mercy of someone else's interpretation of your piece, it can also be illuminating. Another conductor may show you something in your music that you've never heard before. I've been surprised to hear, when someone else conducts my music, how lyric and melodic it can be. It is rare, of course, for a young composer to be able to count on conducting his or her work. Nevertheless, I suggest that you prepare a way of showing, with gestures, time signatures and dynamics, since you may be called on to give them. I've experienced a dry mouth and knocking knees as a studio full of Local 802 musicians waited for me to give the downbeat. I've watched horn players exchange smirks when I couldn't coordinate the tasks of keeping time, indicating dynamics, and bringing one of them in on his solo. Trial by humiliation is not always the best method of learning, and furthermore, it's possible you will lose crucial aspects of your music if you can't give out the clear signals of an informed leader.

Beyond being a useful practical skill, conducting can be an inspiration to the composer, a source of power that can be fed back into the music. The first time you lift up your arm and a sound occurs, the feeling is extraordinary. Or perhaps you give an upbeat, and the whole orchestra enters on the downbeat. It's like breathing for the first time, and that breath rings with incredible sounds.

Whether I conduct or not, the first moment my music gets played, after so much solitary imagining and constructing, is an experience unlike any other. When the sounds I've loved since childhood come together as a mature creative expression—organized, pleasing, powerful, and vivid—I feel affirmed and purposeful. I am also empowered to fight all the difficulties that lie before me in this infuriating and heartbreaking vocation. However, I'm aware that during long dry spells, in which no one has used my services or music, or has had a kind word to say about my past, I've been no less inspired by sounds or impelled to write music. This inspiration, beyond everything else, moves me to keep working at my craft by collecting the lore and skills that will take my music to its next creative place.

FOUR

Basic Training

WHERE AND HOW DOES ONE BEST LEARN the practical skills that I've been discussing? There are several ways, and your choice will most likely be influenced by the kind of music that interests you. The conservatory—places like Juilliard, Eastman, Curtis, Mannes—offers one kind of training. In this setting, students are dedicated solely to the study of music, and the emphasis is on the classical tradition. You are not encouraged to be a "professional" until you graduate; on the other hand, you must be virtually a professional to be accepted in the first place. The emphasis in a conservatory is music history and theory and conventional performance techniques and strategies. In most conservatories, the prevailing view of what musical art is is orthodox and may leave little room for a more eclectic approach.

A student who attends a conservatory is exposed to strict opinions, schedules, assignments. He or she will be critiqued by professors and fellow students. The judgments are likely to be fierce because the faculty and student body reflect the elite of the musical culture: the normal student has played an instrument fluently since childhood, understands the names and symbols for musical choices, and is driven by a passion to defend and interpret the past. If a young composer chooses to go to a conservatory, she will be exposed to the kind of discipline that enforces and expands solid technique and theoretical knowledge. With the high level of expectation and accomplishment come competitiveness, stress, and an illusion that there are no possibilities other than those acceptable to the insulated world of classical music. The conservatory student is generally independent, competitive, interested in scholarly detail, and inspired by the traditional masters.

I am not a classically trained composer, but I have many friends who are. Though I would have suffocated and failed in the conservatory environment, my friends say they would have been paralyzed by my eclectic, haphazard, mobile musical education. I don't believe in being judgmental about such choices. You have to try what suits your musical voice and personal temperament. Franz Liszt once played one of his Hungarian rhapsodies for a grand dinner at the royal court. There was a full Gypsy orchestra in attendance to supply dancing music for the guests. After Liszt played the rhapsody, the leader of the orchestra, deeply moved, asked Liszt if his musicians could honor the composer by playing back what they'd just heard. The Gypsies thereupon performed the whole rhapsody by ear in an improvised but full orchestral arrangement. This is what Gypsy musicians could do, having lived off their wits playing and living music since childhood. I can't imagine musical history without Liszt or a musical world without gypsy musicians. Often a young composer may have to try different methods of learning the craft before deciding if she wants to be a gypsy, Liszt, or some personal combination of the two.

I know a composer who is now involved in creating operas with acoustic instruments, rock and roll doo-wop voices, and a symphonic orchestra produced by a Synclavier. He's full of mischief and loves to slip puns and crazy sound effects alongside very intense (and, I believe, beautiful) meditations on nature and mythical journeys (his most recent work revolves around Joyce's *Ulysses*). When I first met him in Buffalo, we were both thirteen and he was a classical pianist who worshiped Mozart. He played recitals and set his interpretations of Kahlil Gibran's *The Prophet* and Edna St. Vincent Millay's sonnets in stiffly romantic forms. He attended Buffalo's conservative prep school and was intent on getting in to Juilliard.

When we were sixteen, Thelonious Monk came to Buffalo's Royal Arms' jazz club, and his brilliant technique and quirky, free-form interpretations of melody quickly inspired us all. My friend, however, became obsessed. He started practicing jazz, listening to jazz, hanging around jazz musicians at SUNY-Buffalo, and his art songs turned into piano solos with blues-inspired progressions. He continued to study classical piano, theory, and history, and prepared for his Juilliard audition, but his conflicting interest in jazz grew stronger. He wanted to know all the technical devices of composing (he still loved Mozart). He thought he wanted to write opera, but he couldn't stay away from jazz. When he was accepted at Juilliard, he decided to go there, but he spent most of his nights going to jazz clubs. After a year, he flunked out of the conservatory and decided he'd learn the craft of a jazz composer by creating a group and playing. However, my friend, though an imaginative composer, was not an improvisational musician. He needed the control of the written page, and though inspired by harmonics and rhythms of Monk and Parker, he really didn't want to make music that way. After another unhappy year of waiting tables and fighting with his group, he decided to go to the Berklee College of Music in Boston, where he could study jazz theory and history in the security of an academic setting, while maintaining his contacts with an urban jazz environment.

My friend needed to soak up academic opinions about the forms of music that moved him. In time, he began to use synthesizers in his creation of jazz-influenced rhythms and riffs, and transferred to Stanford University, which has a top electronic music department. When he returned to New York, he quickly connected himself to the growing number of composers exploring synthesizers at Columbia University. He claims to feel most at ease while taking in a concert at the Blue Note, or singing along with Motown revivals at the Bottom Line (a cabaret in New York), but he thrives on the intellectual back and forth of academic music. I believe his compositions work because they are rooted in a well-cultivated classical background. The conservatory, then, can be an enabling place for the person who needs to base his work on a tradition. Also, to be able to hear a piece of music and analyze it with a fluid, educated ear must provide the same kind of mental power as knowing how all the parts come together to make a rocket take off. Conservatories try to cultivate a real respect for musicianship. They are expensive, but do offer scholarship programs for talented students regardless of sex or race.

Another possibility is to enroll in a liberal arts college or university and major in music. Your musical education in this setting may be similar to that offered by the conservatory, but you will also, especially in the first years, be exposed to other disciplines: history, philosophy, literature, science. Music is not the entire raison d'être in such schools. You encounter other kinds of artistic tastes, and you have a bit more of a life. All schools are not equal, of course, and the danger in this choice is that you may not get the kind of classical background you must have if you're going to involve yourself in complex orchestrating and notating. So choose carefully. Make sure the music department is a strong one. Oberlin, the University of Chicago, and Columbia are among several schools that offer versatile academic programs and have strong music departments.

The type of character who thrives in this academic environment is a serious student who wants to acquire an excellent background in several fields. This person would want to know, for example, about Elizabethan and Jacobean drama, eighteenth-century French painting, and the major aesthetic philosophers as well as music theory. Interested in music's place among the arts, he believes that a good artist has to be steeped in cultural history.

A composer, then, should examine the nature of his talent, interests, and temperament in the course of pursuing a musical education. I know a young woman, now twenty-two, who started writing musicals at the age of thirteen in Philadelphia, where she became recognized for her prodigious output. She studied classical composition at the University of Pennsylvania with George Crumb, but her ambition to "do Broadway" brought her to New York and New York University. NYU is the kind of college that offers ambitious young people academic support while they go out and make professional connections. This young woman is currently setting up her second full musical workshop in two years. She has access to an NYU theater space and advisers who will critique her final product. She's primarily interested in getting funding support, commercial producers, and production experience. She listens to the advice of a smart investor with the same attention she gives to a prestigious professor of baroque harmony.

Because of their proximity to the music business, schools like NYU and UCLA are excellent for composers who are interested in show business but want the security of a campus. These schools are different from Juilliard or Eastman, whose students no doubt have equal longings to have their works performed, but feel an obligation to acquire the academic résumés that help them do battle for commissions and contests after graduation. Students who go to both types of schools generally have decided to bypass college life in favor of making an investment toward a professional career. My most recent contact with student composers verifies my suspicion that most are there to learn how to be successful and not to explore the directions their talent might take. I wish conservatories and music departments would de-emphasize the vocational aspect of art and help students understand the value of rest, time, observation, and even play.

The "artsy" schools, such as Hampshire, Bennington, Antioch, Cal Arts, SUNY Purchase to a degree, are valuable, I think, for students who want to experiment not just with the content and forms of music but with its *use*. Since I am a graduate of Bennington, I can speak firsthand of its dedication to combining composition with dance, theater, and poetry. The term "crossover," so popular now, can be traced back to the Martha Graham era at Bennington when dance, drama, design, and music merged. I remember my first vocal experiments with an improvisational dancer, Lisa Nelson. She danced down a long hallway of the new science laboratory while I provided four variations on the Beatles' tune "Help." This kind of work could easily drown in its own pretentiousness were it not for the bracing sense of standards brought by the faculty in these institutions. In a college where life, art, and work are thought to be one, and where commercial and even academic ambitions are scorned in favor of "true discovery," each day matters.

A student who chooses such a college should be genuinely drawn to new forms, not be easily seduced by the musical marketplace, and possess a strong inner drive. The discipline at schools like Bennington, Hampshire, and Cal Arts is expected to come from within. Their professors can provide as thorough an academic background as anywhere, but they expect their students to explore and create on their own. The dangers of these schools are that they encourage a retreat into oneself and that their loose schedules and guidance are hard for some young people, who feel lonely and disoriented. A young composer who thrives at an arts college is likely to live very much in the present and to realize that experimentation moves forward in fits and fragments, often coming together only later in life as an acceptable form.

During my time at Bennington, there were regular rehearsals of thirty or more cellists who specialized in playing new compositions, and around the clock musical theater involving, say, rock and roll, anti-Vietnam literature, folk and ethnic sounds, and new dance. Composers worked with architects and sculptors to create new environments and instruments. Dancers performed choreography written out by composers and other dancers. Arts colleges encourage their young composers to know the classics, to respect form, and to be cognizant of historical precedents in experimentation, but they mainly benefit the serious students who need to follow their idiosyncratic muses early on.

Some composers (particularly songwriters) may do best to choose a college for its strengths in other fields as well as the arts and regard music mainly as an extracurricular activity. These are the composers who need to soak up the world around them—sports, politics, parties, lectures, the town outside the college—and perceive their composing as closely related to "real life." Charles Ives literally suffered through his composition courses at Yale, and a young composer with a similar temperament might find his talents best put to use by writing songs for a fraternity skit or putting together a revue to protest campus policy. A friend of mine, who now writes movie scores, began his career at the University of Michigan, where he was a drill sergeant in the ROTC and composed satirical music for the campus cabaret.

Some people learn music mostly by playing it in a band, jazz ensemble, or folk group. A situation that requires you to deal with all the logistics of carting and setting up instruments, speakers, and amps and to think about what you're going to play to capture the audience's attention, how to get paid, and how to get ahead can be enormously educational. The members of U2 aren't college educated; the Beatles didn't finish high school; Duke Ellington didn't attend a conservatory. Most jazz and rock composers learn their craft in bars and clubs and on the road. The drawback to this is that you play only your own music, or the music that fits the instruments of your band.

I emphasized earlier how important it is for a composer to become acquainted with the widest possible range of instruments and kinds of music. Defining yourself narrowly too early can stunt your musical growth. However, playing with several different kinds of groups can add up to an effective musical education. I know a musician who played oboe for NYU movie scores, played saxophone in a rock group, subbed in a big band, and practiced classical flute in a chamber ensemble. He also played several instruments in an experimental theater ensemble, where he gradually began to come into his own as a composer. If you choose to learn this way, explore several options, not just one, and keep changing as the music around you extends your composing vocabulary.

Another way to learn about music is to work in a musical environment even if you're not playing. This is especially valuable to a composer like me, who is inspired as much by the characters of the performers as by the scope of their music. "Hanging out" is a way of taking in music history and theory. You can watch how and why performers choose certain keys; how one tune can be interpreted several different ways; how different types of bands use crescendos, modulations, orchestration. I'll never forget being a guest during a session where Leon Redbone was cutting a tune with just an acoustic guitar and a tuba. I'd never heard the possibilities for a tuba in quite such a humorous but lyric way. A young composer with a fiction writer's temperament might want to work in a club or a concert hall, collecting tickets, handing out programs, scrubbing floors, washing windows. I know a lot of fine musicians who started out as ushers at the New York East Side rock club Filmore East. I've worked in the La Mama box office, at the Café Lena in Saratoga Springs, and in the office of Pete Seeger's Hudson sloop *Clearwater*, which drew attention to environmental issues. In none of these places was I asked to share any of my great musical ideas, nor was I invited to contribute any of my music. But I stuck around and I learned.

If you're with people who are creating music and you're paying attention, you can learn what makes a piece of music work and what doesn't. Something works when the composer's intention is completed in rhythm, harmony, emotion, overtone, and energy. If a solid little machine is created that doesn't break down in the middle, doesn't lose its springs, doesn't run out of gas before it's supposed to, and doesn't speed up and crash into a wall, then it works. Hanging out, and watching people come and go, you will see this happen and you will also see it not happen. Nothing is more educational than failure, as you will learn with your own. But first, watch the people you admire fall down. Watch how they learn to laugh at themselves. Watch how they pick themselves up and try again.

Obviously, the hanging-out school of musical education has its limitations. There are many practical skills that you can't learn this way. It's easy to lose track of the reason you're there, to forget about actually writing music. Late hours and getting caught up in the scene can undermine the discipline you need to function as a composer. I wouldn't recommend this approach for more than a year or so. But if you stay aware of the secret you're carrying inside while you're acting as an observer, you can pick up valuable knowledge.

I discussed the benefits of learning by apprenticeship in the last chapter. If you make this your primary educational mode, you should also be aware that it can have drawbacks. Chances are your musical world will be as great or as small as that of the composer with whom you're associated. Should he happen to be, say Aaron Copland, whose world is a rich one, you will be fortunate. The trade-off for being associated with someone well-known is that you risk becoming known as his or her pupil for life. On the other hand, if you hook up with someone who has difficulty getting his or her music played, someone who is not well grounded in the practicalities of a musical life, you will suffer from a jaundiced and narrow outlook.

Young people with open minds don't inspect their mentors' résumés. Nor are they likely to analyze personalities. Hooking on to a charismatic misanthrope who has little good to say about the rest of the world because of her own fears, misadventures, or lack of talent can teach you a kind of bitterness that discourages developing strong, hard-won opinions. I'm always careful not be be fooled by the type of composer who's brilliantly articulate in a sour, grudging manner toward everyone but a close circle of friends. This temperament can easily be covering a lazy or damaged person who has simply given up.

Whatever method of learning you choose, it should be a rigorous one. Music, like athletics, requires strenuous and sustained training. Without it, you become superficial, inefficient, weak, and limited.

Another invaluable part of a young composer's education is travel. You don't have to buy camping gear, hitch a ride on a freighter, and wander from youth hostel to youth hostel unless that's your style. I know of many college choirs who have traveled through Europe, Asia, and the Middle East. Foundations offer exchange programs. The ethnomusicology departments at Wesleyan and Cal Arts introduce interested students to masters of music from Japan, Bali, West Africa, and India. Such contacts can often lead to invitations back and forth. However you can manage it, travel is invaluable in expanding your musical vocabulary. A composer interested in chorale work should not miss Soviet Georgian choral singing, which begins with simple, sustained notes and then breaks into harmonies and chord changes completely foreign to the Western ear. An adventurous trek to the Negev can bring you the sounds of nomad boys beating out 7/8 rhythms on a gasoline can. Traveling to third world nations where there is poverty and famine and crisis teaches that music is not a luxury but a need, and that real music is made under all kinds of circumstances.

In Nicaragua and El Salvador, one might encounter Catholic feast days. The combination of Indian and Hispanic folk songs with religious hymns is beautiful. In Cambodia, the play songs of the children are spare and haunting, with unfamiliar intervals and rhythms. The political folk music of Chile has a new dramatic substance, which carries both the message of its lyrics and the fervor of drums and guitars. In South Africa, the polyphonic choral singing has proved to be a source of power to the blacks fighting apartheid. In Africa and other nations suffering from AIDS and political upheaval, ritual drumming and ceremony goes on as best it can to celebrate the births, deaths, and rites of passage of its people. Music is a necessary connection to cultural heritage and to the expression of love within families. However raw this music may be, there is nothing simplistic about it. Like prayer, it comes from the human need to survive, and to express and pass on life's celebratory and tragic experiences.

The minimalists, like Steve Reich and Philip Glass and Terry Riley, who are currently so popular in our culture, owe a great deal to the sounds of India and Asia. African music, of course, is a powerful influence on Western rock and jazz. Paul Simon in *Graceland* introduced the rich bushland vocal harmonies to mainstream rock, and in so doing revitalized his career. The pentatonic scale has found its way into many compositions by New Age artists such as George Winston and his group of Windham Hill artists. Michael Jackson and Quincy Jones bring to their catchy synthesized drum tracks hypnotizing beats like those in Brazilian *capoeira* dancing. Miles Davis is a master of exotic music, his trumpet moving from the blue riffs of black American music to styles of African and Brazilian song and chant. So are Herbie Hancock and Chick Corea. The Police epitomize a youthful white adaptation of black reggae. I have a friend who composes masses in south Indian ragas and another who uses the clicks and mouth percussion of East Africa to accentuate her personal rock and roll scat style.

For a composer to assimilate the music of a foreign culture, there must be something more than an anthropological recreation of it. Usually the culture itself has to be experienced and assimilated with his own background and personality. Otherwise a composer is like a forger who turns valuable relics into airport art. Most cultures connect their music to religion and other rites of passion, and to make a genuine use of it requires an act of the soul.

Some years ago, I was the composer for a theater company that was touring West Africa. Crossing the Sahara Desert, we were surrounded by waves of sand and a broad sky and a silence so pure that when the wind rose up I could hear the chords hidden in it. Then one day we stopped for lunch. I was startled to hear in the midst of this silence the sound of a flute, played with a breathy tone reminiscent of the desert wind. I followed the sound. About one hundred yards from our campsite, I came upon the player: a dark-skinned man with Indian features, tattooed cheeks, and leather bracelets on both wrists, wrapped in a tattered indigo cloth, and sitting on saddlebags dyed deep red, sea green, and black. He was playing a small, hand-carved nose flute. When he saw me and grinned, a mouth full of bright orange teeth told me he was a Tuareg (a tribe that uses an orange root for a toothbrush).

We began to speak in broken French, and I learned that his asthma interfered with his breathing and caused him to go off-key. He patiently taught me a few phrases on the flute and didn't object to my scribbling down on my lunch napkin the simple mode on which he'd been improvising. (If I remember correctly, he played a repeated cycle of two high E's, two G's, two F-sharps, a C below, and back to the two E's. His irregular breathing bent each cycle of the pattern into different quarter tones and accents.) Soon after, I left him curled under a bush in the midday sun, playing his soft, slightly wheezing music over and over like a Mideastern calliope. His sounds were unique; I would never have heard them in any other situation, nor would the experience have mattered much if I hadn't given myself up to it.

I've already mentioned the talking drums in Nigeria that speak poetry, that holler directions at the dancers, that tell stories. They may relate the history of someone who has just entered that room, telling of his forefathers, what he likes to wear or eat, even whom he has fought with or made love to, how much gold he has, what birds sang in the trees the day he married. You may not know what the drum is actually saying, but you will hear its voice, its intonation, and its flawless sense of phrasing. You can learn from it that nothing is more important to composition than phrasing. A composer, like a writer, needs to be able to speak with his or her music. Phrases should have a clear beginning, middle, and end, and connect with each other in a distinct and purposeful way. They should not meander arbitrarily or fade out or drop. The talking drums provide a splendid example of such structure.

The urgent sense of melody in the vocal singing I encountered in Africa also helped me to discover my present way of using voice in musical theater. The singing has an immediate and practical function: it conjures the night, cajoles the sun, summons the rain, speaks to the sand. It warns young children of what is about to happen. It praises the elders for helping the village to prosper and promoting its spiritual well-being. The storyteller's voice acts out many different parts. It's like hearing a ventriloquist, an impressionist, a child singer, a mother singing a lullaby, an animal tamer, a lover, a sports announcer, and so forth performed by the same person in a controlled trance. We are not accustomed to such a virtuoso use of the voice, since much of our everyday association with language has deteriorated to listening to the literal meanings of words rather than the sounds and rhythms of each vowel, consonant, and pitch.

African choral singing also offers a new sound to the Western ear because no one is trying to sing beautifully (though, I must say, the result is beautiful). The singers' purpose is not to create a perfectly shaped tone as in Western opera, but rather to sing the song, a purpose that originates in a deep place within the singers. They are not separated from their music as we are from ours as something only professionals do seriously. They don't get dressed up on Saturday night and go to a building to watch talented people engage in this activity. They don't separate the artists from people who sing for a hobby. The music is an organic part of daily life, which by definition makes it less precious, less studied. It occurs naturally, and this creates a completely different sound. It's not a better sound. The tension and ceremony that accompany the Western gospel choir or blues band provide a thrill that is undeniable. But African singing is a different experience that was profoundly important for me to encounter and understand.

Soon after my return from Africa, I set a number of Sylvia Plath's *Ariel* poems to music. I found when I worked on "Daddy" or "Lady Lazurus"—two poems that express their rage in a chanted circular meter with rough stops and coarse vowels—I was as much concerned with the interpretation of the sounds as with the literal meaning of the words. I didn't try to illustrate the movements of each line with a melodic underscore. I used three or four notes a line, allowing the sounds of the words themselves to create tension and conflict. Therefore, I had to practice a special pronunciation, which, though not a dialect, became a crucial part of the musical composition. The striking of *t*'s, the guttural emphasis of *gl, k,* and *y,* as well as the conscious manipulation of *D* in "Daddy" became an integral part of the scoring. Whenever I sang the songs myself or taught them to anyone else, these "pronunciations" were as essential to the music as the melodic notes and measures of time.

As I've continued to explore the use of the voice as an instrument, one passion has led me to adapt classical Greek tragedies. In *Medea, Elektra,* and *The Trojan Women,* I used the double *o* sounds and *gh* diphthongs as musical choices in themselves. I rearranged the roots of certain words as if they were instruments. By repeating a syllable like *tcha,* I could be fierce and percussive; I could turn *ai ai* into calling and lamentation. I've also invented a sound language for Pharoah and his Wizards in *The Haggadah,* tried to capture the sound of the streets in the beats, consonants, and vowels of kids, and made a theater piece from prerevolutionary Russian poetry readings of Mandelstam, Akhmatova, Tsvetaeva, and the great basso Mayakovski.

All of my theater pieces are heightened and articulated by choruses singing in raw, straightforward harmonies. The soloist tells his or her story and is then swallowed by a rush of reactions from multiple voices. My experiences with African rituals have given me the desire and means to fill a stage with the most energy I can concentrate by layering drums and voices; by contrasting whispering solos with the crash of a signaling gong, a violent piano with a hummed chord. I want my melodic lines to be much more energetic than memorable combinations of notes. The sound of the words are part of the melody; the husk or lilt of the singers' voices fosters the aura of mystery. I want nothing I do to be mere effect. If I could afford it, I'd spend months in workshop making sure every performer understood exactly how to taste a word, speak with a drum, elaborate and fuse with the action as an instrumentalist does. I continue to be less drawn to the *concertizing* aspects of much Western musical life than I am to music as ritual.

The point here is not to imitate the sounds of another country, a pitfall that many, myself included, fell into in the late sixties and early seventies when gaggles of Jewish, WASP, and Catholic college kids with permed Afros and wrapped in dashikis or saris carried around exotically carved instruments and played them as if they were clones rather than young composers influenced by the music of other cultures. You don't want to do this any more than you want to imitate Handel. Imitation will only produce phony ethnic writing. But you do want to understand why the music of another culture works, and if you have that understanding, you can translate it into your own work.

This new pespective will also provoke you to ask of your own music, what is its human value? What can it mean to your fellow human beings? For what reason was it composed?

Of course, many rituals are shared by all cultures: births, rites of passage, weddings, deaths. But even in these instances the role of emotion, and its musical reflection, will vary widely. Once in Africa I heard ethereal, angelic music coming from a distant forest. There were flutes, bells, very high voices, and lightly tapping drums. I followed the sound and came to a clearing where young children were dancing like birds in front of a hut. A crowd gathered and sang a chorus every now and then. Then a body wrapped in muslin was brought out of the hut. It was a funeral, but very different from the Orthodox Jewish funeral, with its grief-laden melodies and cries, or the wailing and keening of an Irish wake, or the mysterious, distanced chanting of the Koran in the Middle East.

Other cultures also have a much more direct connection between their instruments and the environment in which they live than we do. In northern Nigeria, I often saw little boys walking around playing what we would call a thumb piano, though it bore no resemblance to our version. It was made from the bamboo trees of the region, and its sound was unique. Consider the difference between playing a one-of-a-kind instrument carved from a holy tree in Africa and strumming a factory-produced guitar.

The information and impressions that you gather from traveling, the rich musical vocabulary to which you're exposed, whether or not you draw on it directly, are also their own reward. It's simply wonderful to know these things, to have heard these sounds. They are reasons to be alive.

The relationship in other cultures between politics and music often is much stronger, and more specific, than it is in the United States. When Shostakovich refused to follow Stalin's musical taste, he was abused. The hands of the Chilean composer/folksinger Victor Jara were broken in the infamous stadium in Santiago during the repression of 1970 before he was murdered. In El Salvador today, young radicals use traditional folk melodies to set political texts as well as writing their own tunes. Political music is coming out of Ireland, Syria, Lebanon, Israel, much of it advocating peace and expressing a hope that new generations may move away from old grudges. In any country that is in a state of transition and upheaval, such as South Africa or Nicaragua, you may be sure that music will play a part in the struggle.

American music also reflects its political influences. The work and gospel songs of Southern slaves, which eventually grew into the blues, expressed the misery and hopes of a life without freedom. Many of the love songs of these same black Americans, once they were freed, spoke not just of a man and woman searching for each other but of the agony of a race decimated by the whims and greed of another race. American Yiddish music, particularly that written during the years of the Holocaust, often embodied the guilt and concern toward those left behind. The music of the sixties and early seventies was laden with opposition to racism, militarism, and capitalism.

It is also true that subtle forms of censorship exist in American musical life, as a result of economic barriers and cultural biases that deny the value of certain musical traditions. The popular music industry in the United States is governed solely by the profit-making motive. Independent record producers—Angel, Caedmon, Nonesuch—and alternative music performing groups are often in frequent financial jeopardy because the control of the industry is in the hands of the major labels, which pay radio stations to play their music and record stores to display their albums prominently. The current administration has cut back on its support of music and the other arts. But while our musicians do have these problems, America does not throw them in jail and torture them (those who maintain that we do so metaphorically are hysterics who devalue the suffering of artists in truly repressive systems).

Young artists often have a tendency to ignore whatever lies beyond the narrow boundaries of their own experience. This problem is perhaps even greater for people working in nonverbal art forms. It is easy to become so absorbed in combining notes, making harmonies, experimenting with pure sound, or writing songs for the sake of creating a character or for getting people on their feet and dancing that you forget the existence of the broad musical spectrum.

For this reason, I give students exercises meant to wipe out their preconceived notions of music and set free their musical imaginations. Often I begin with the voice and ask my students to learn many different vocal styles from many different cultures. Perhaps they learn Gregorian chant, a ritual song from Mali, and how to harmonize in the doo-wop style of the Supremes.

I might teach a narrative line from Noh drama or a vocal drumming off the tabla. As a student experiences different ways of making sound with the body, her body loosens up. When the fear of using your own instrument is lessened, your mind becomes more open. You listen differently. You can absorb a greater quantity of sounds without intellectualization. A composer must always be open to expanding her vocabulary.

I also encourage my students to imitate animal voices; one group of students might create a "chorale" bassed on barnyard sounds, another on animals in the jungle. I want my overly serious students to understand the many levels of play. When children play, they are very serious, but their imaginations are as yet unfettered by opinions of what is good and bad play. Therefore, their sounds are fully committed. Their imaginary stories follow a true internal rhythm. As we get older, we absorb unconscious rules and censors. It's important for a young composer to find ways to break down intellectual censorship to play. Animal sounds are as pure and free a way of opening up the voice as I have found. Birds and insects appear in many genres of musical composition and are also the models for many instruments. In Latin music, the güiro produces a sound reminiscent of crickets. The Brazilian cuika can sound just like a frog. *Peter and the Wolf* is filled with animal voices made by Western instruments. It's important for the young composer to become reacquainted with the natural sounds of various instruments, just as she first discovered at an early age, perhaps through *Peter and the Wolf* or *Tubby the Tuba* or Benjamin Britten's *Young Person's Guide to the Orchestra*, that each instrument's raw sound imitates a voice from a natural world.

I encourage a kind of childlike imagination in my students in other ways. I want them to see that a trumpet not only covers so many notes but also has a certain personality or character, a certain timbre. Many other cultures believe that instruments have spirits, and they are treated with care and respect. I discuss with my students the possibilties of Western instruments having spirits, and I reduce the discussion to roughly kindergarten level because the more childlike one can be, the more effective the exercise. Is someone living inside the instrument? Does that someone have a name? A corporeal form? A characteristic activity? I recall a student who envisioned gnomes, with long gray beards and grumbling voices, living inside a timpani and performing as trapeze artists, hitting their heads and landing in nets. It's fine for a nineteen-year-old to talk for a day in this mythic, storytelling way about an instrument; you can rest assured he or she will never forget the association, and his or her feeling for the instrument will be deepened.

I mentioned early that music in most other cultures is an intrinsic part of ceremonial and daily life. I ask my students to create a ritual, to name it, to think about the instrumentation, a song that might be part of the ceremony, a dance. This may be devised for an imaginary country or a real one. A perennial favorite among students living in New York City is the cockroach purification rite, almost invariably a flamenco dance number in rap music time.

A young jazz pianist invented a "late night welfare hotel tango." He took the cover off the baseboard, slammed on the open strings, shouted into the piano's open body, and demonstrated with his music the violent "rituals" he hears at night. Another student described how, once a year in his country, the rain changed to a sweet cleansing oil, and all the citizens ran out and slapped it onto their bodies. This turned into a drum solo all over his body: a rock version of hambone.

Creating a ritual awakens the kind of inspiration that is a source of composition, a connection to the unfolding of days and seasons and the other passages of time. It emphasizes the potential for celebration in the events around us. I also encourage students to bring a sense of humor into play in this exercise because young people tend to be overly serious; they will find plenty of opportunities to indulge that inclination, but the chance to learn to laugh at themselves is harder to come by. Also, if you don't begin to do that as composer, you risk becoming habituated to expressing false emotional extremes such as grief, rage, joy.

I also use a series of exercises I call Betty Crockers, which require the student to compose a piece of music in ten minutes: two lines of a song, or a vocal rendition of an instrumental solo, or a three-part harmony background doo-wop, with a clear, precise beginning, middle, and end. In another variation, I ask students to examine the room and quickly find an object that will serve as an instrument: an empty chair, garbage can, comb, radiator. This is your only voice; learn what it can do and write for its particular range. Still another variation is what I call the "ten minute opera," in which a student is to select a partner, pick a conflict or resolution of a conflict, put together a few lines of dialogue, improvise singing off that exchange, and then set the notes. As students learn to work in a group with an absolute, ridiculously short deadline, they learn a lot about the trade of commercial composing.

At the time of this writing, I've taken on a job writing a movie score that will be recorded in two weeks. I have eighteen cues to write and orchestrate that will fit with exactly timed pieces of film footage. I must learn Puerto Rican music so that it sounds as though I grew up with it and incorporate it into a non-Latin score; book musicians and a studio; rehearse and record . . . all of this on a low budget, and while I'm working on another score. If I weren't able to spread myself out in these ways, I wouldn't be able to support myself writing music. Big pieces like *Jerusalem* or *The Beautiful Lady*, the work for musical theater based on the Russian Acmeists, the pieces that offer me emotional sustenance, musically speaking, do not pay the bills. Work that does usually has a deadline, and most often it's harrowing for other reasons. If you freeze under that kind of pressure, you're lost, and it's unlikely that you'll be able to survive as a composer.

Another Betty Crocker that forces students to learn how to work under time pressure is the one I call a lying workshop. I give an assignment, let's say writing a chorus of a silly song about trees in bliss, to be completed in one minute. Since they cannot finish it in that time, they write it in effect while they're performing for me. What they're really doing is improvising on the spot, but I call it lying to diminish the overly sacred connotations that go with the word "improvise." I can't overstate the importance of developing this skill. If you find yourself, for instance, recording a film score, or working in a theatrical situation, you will have to be able to redo an orchestration or a melody or a line of counterpoint on the spot. The producer has forgotten what he asked you for. "Would you please explain one more time what it was you wanted?" you ask, smiling, then rewrite in your head while he's explaining, and then execute on the spot this latest idea, even though it's competely different from the one he had the day before. I have had the experience of recording a film score with the director hanging over my shoulder, telling me as I was conducting the live orchestra that he wanted certain changes, and I've changed entire cues without stopping: in mid-recording, speeding up, slowing down, conducting half the instruments out, bringing others in. It's true that I sometimes felt like I was ready for the hospital at day's end, but it was also an incredible challenge.

Can you change a 1940s swing harmony to a 1960s sound in five seconds? Can you make instant allowances and move from a Renaissance sound to a baroque one? Can you switch from country-western to bluegrass, fast? Can you create a sense of mysterious music that then moves into something terrifying because the producers have decided to cut an additional five minutes of footage from the film? I've often thrown out five or six songs in a show because the producers asked me to. If I think they're wrong, and the cuts are destructive to the work, I'll fight with all the temperament I can muster. If I think they have a point, I'll cut (and promise myself that I'll find a place for them somewhere else. One song has traveled through at least five shows before it finally found a home.) I'll do the job I was hired to do.

Along with this highly developed adaptiveness, it also helps to have a sense of humor. Ultimately, of course, what matters is your own music that you create for yourself, but there will be time for that, and you can grow soft sitting at home, endlessly thinking about it. You will not be corrupted by practicing your trade in a workmanlike way by learning to think of your feet. You will, in fact, develop a kind of musical flexibility that will feed your future compositions.

Betty Crockers also teach a young composer to collaborate, and under difficult conditions. Music is by nature a collaborative art, and the sooner you can learn to handle this gracefully, the better. Despite my earlier descriptions of composers' temperaments, those moments of madness every artist suffers, collaboration requires open-mindedness and fast thinking. The quicker the access a composer has to his or her wellsprings of technique the more likely musical problems can be solved without bruised egos, misunderstandings, and misplaced power trips. I believe that one of the terrible problems of the current musical theater is how unwilling each individual creator is to change his or her ideas for the sake of the success of the whole production.

Another exercise I use is to have students set an unlikely text to music, emphasis on *unlikely*. Maybe it's the "People" page of *Time* magazine, or a page from an almanac on next year's weather, or the proverbial page from the phone book. I encourage the students to do whatever they can to give musical life to these essentially lifeless texts, and they learn in the course of this exercise that little happens if they simply impose their own point of view—humorous, tragic, ironic, angry, joyful—on the text. However, if they let the written word, no matter how boring or strange, work with the music, if they utilize the energy of what exists on the page, the result is much more satisfactory. Emotion must be specific to work. A general application of a vague notion of happy, sad, or funny isn't lively because those words are summations for very specific emotional moments with thousands of nuances. If the word "Idaho" is worked on for its long *I,* its short *da,* its open *o,* chances are that many memories of experience and emotion will come through (and not necessarily of Idaho). The energy of the commitment to each sound brings forth enough for the ear to deal with, false interpretation being a distraction from the rhythmic and melodic possibilities inspired by studying the word itself. This is comparable to a dancer working with a specific part of her body, not necessarily to lead to a finished work, but to develop clear approaches to movement itself.

Taking this exercise one step further, I ask students to set a favorite poem to music. Listening to such settings, what one first hears is how much the student admires the poem, what she gets or needs from the poem, how the poem relates to her life. What we don't hear is the poem. And that's not good music. Good music reflects and illuminates what exists on the page. The composer's point of view works in conjunction with the words, rather than being imposed upon them.

When I set Pablo Neruda's "Bestiario" to music, I was impressed by the breathless energy of the poet's voice. He lists the animals, birds, and insects of the world that excite him, and the sounds of their names excite him as much as how they move. Every verb and adjective he selects seems to be filled with the physical strangeness of the animals themselves. I saw no need to add my own longings or admiration. Neruda spoke for me, and I tried to accentuate what I love in his poem by finding a theatrical salsa/calypso setting to evoke Central America, syncopations to underline his rushing, uneven meter, and sudden stops to accent his humorous, political punchlines. Point of view in this instance was letting something valuable breathe, or cry, or laugh. (I didn't need to bring other needs into the setting.) This often feels to the young composer like a major renunciation of ego. The truth is quite the opposite, in fact. When you let a great text overtake you, you become the writer of those words; you are the performer, you are the subject of the text; you change parts and attitudes, your adventure is far greater than if you imposed your own single point of view. Your union with a fine writer can be so strong that it takes a while to come down and remember the work existed before you laid your hands on it.

In another difficult, related exercise, a student has to write a piece of music, whose structure uses unconventional tonalities and either unusual instruments or common instruments in an unusual way, for someone else in the class to perform. Students write eight to sixteen measures of music and notate it in a way that is easy to follow. I don't stress the unusual for the sake of weirdness but to disassociate the student from habitual ways of composing and hearing. By disorienting him or her, the exercise helps the young composer begin to listen in a new way. I want students to learn how to notate a drum that is trying to talk, for example, or a piccolo that is gasping like a tardy bird rushing south to escape winter. Students relish the opportuntity to write for each other, to allow their imaginations free rein and to exercise the visual aspect of their consciousness.

Music can be, literally, a way of talking, as the following exercise demonstrates. Divide a dialogue between a percussion instrument and a person speaking rhythmic syllables. The percussionist plays from a written score, the speaker answers; the percussionist plays something more complex, the speaker answers in kind; the dialogue gradually becomes more intricate and urgent. You will hear the difference between a spontaneous, improvisational voice creating rhythms and what you may be forcing upon the drum with your written music. Or, to explore this from a melodic standpoint, uses a flute to take the written part and a voice to improvise responses. Then try writing both parts of the dialogue, two percussion instruments talking to each other, or a violin and a cello, or a violin and a sitar (West meets East). If you have been listening carefully, you will be able to re-create the spontaneous quality of the improvisational voice, and your music will have a new ease, a more organic sense of movement.

Ultimately, you may have three or four instruments on either side of the dialogue. When you do, move the players around. As one group plays, have them sit in chairs, then get up when the other group responds. Now you're exploring not only the dramatic capabilities of the instruments, but how motion and location affect the impact of a line. I ask composers and musicians to move because the "motion" of melodic themes and rhythmic variations shouldn't come from theory alone. Thelonious Monk, during rehearsals of his music, sometimes communicated his desires and comments by dancing an odd, nonstop tap dance. Jazz and rock musicians will often take part in movement exercises without complaint. Classical musicians might resist, as their training doesn't often encourage them to do anything but sit in one place and play. But persevere, because once they let go of their rather rigid procedural notions, they, too, can get up and cooperate.

I try to involve the body in compositional exercises. We may take a Stravinsky or a Schoenberg piece and create a strange folk dance to fit the music. By using the feet, legs, and arms, the whole body comes to understand the life in the 7/8, 3/8, or 5/4 rhythms. (I learned "Stravinsky dancing" from another composer, Vivian Fine.) Then the students write their own rhythmically unpredictable pieces, and create dances for them. The body is involved in writing music, not just the mind and the ears. When I'm working with a company, I spend roughly an hour each day doing strenuous physical work similar to an aerobics class, with an emphasis on listening and responding to improvised sound. I think it's important for a composer to be in good physical shape and to keep the body's channels clean and clear.

I have a variety of exercises to hone students' listening powers, to wake up their ears and minds. One, which seems almost like a party game, is to have everyone close their eyes, while a member of the group walks around and the others try to guess who it is by the sound of the steps. This forces you to develop a keen sense of the other members of the ensemble with whom you're working. Another group exercise is to count together in clapping beats up to sixteen, then clap for eight beats, counting aloud, then clap to eight but say nothing, then stop clapping and say nothing, and all try to clap on eight at the same time. You will feel how each person keeps the internal beat. Who speeds up? Who slows down? Who unconsciously leads the group? I have known ensembles so in tune with one another that they could get up to sixty-four beats, clapping in unison every eight beats, then removing the claps and, in complete silence, clapping on sixty-four at exactly the same time.

Studying Indian raga, with its quarter tones, causes one to listen to the notes that are in between our twelve notes. Singing the national anthem with every note a quarter tone flat or sharp, as the late avant-garde soprano Cathy Berberian taught me to do, introduces your ear to a technique for creating sounds that are humorous as well as sour, or otherwise strange or interesting. Rhythmic chanting with solo voices piling on top of one another is a good way to understand the concept of building rhythmic patterns that underlies the music of many Latin and African ensembles.

When I work with New Wave or conceptual artists, I use exercises that force them to move from expositional writing to a more intelligent theatrical mode. Many cheap rock and roll songs simply talk about a state of being: "I'm hurting from the loss of your loving, baby—bring it on back to me." This kind of writing is akin to a bad monologue where emotions and events are infantilized and reduced to a formula. It is possible, of course, for ballads to express mature emotion in a convincing way. I grew up on such ballads and believe the strength of rock and roll lies in its emotional immediacy. However, unless the composer learns to reveal emotional experience through time, using hidden meanings and imaginative detail, the strong feelings she wishes to express soon become banal. When these explosions of feeling are combined with confessional lyrics and a wailing performance, it can be a truly cathartic experience. But harmony and development must be combined with energy and concept for a composer to go past adolescent fantasies of pain, passion, existential bitterness, and youthful violence.

MTV is loaded with tunes that are based on this kind of face-forward presentational imagery, and a little of it goes a long way. An artist should be able to make a choice between expository writing and writing that is at once more dramatic and abstract. I ask these artists to write a rock and roll song. It can be as funky or hard-core or mellow or funny as they like, but it must be from the point of view of a character. And the music must be about that specific character, not about being that song.

I ask composers to write lyrics, even if ultimately they have no intention of being lyricists (or even if they're uninterested in vocal music). Song is the heart of most music, and words are part of song, not a separate element added on. I ask them to write their lyrics about one tiny detail of a lover's face. Lyrics devoted to the eyes will require focused music. Lyrics speaking about one branch of a tree require a concentration that a composer will not get from trying to summarize the Massachusetts–New York border in autumn. Sometimes a student responds cynically, with the humor typical of a generation short on poetry and too full of late-night TV satire. Satire is fine, but it, too, must be specific. If the student makes fun of the assignment by writing a choral ode to a pimento, I point out that the ode would be more humorous if the student knew more about the pimento. Broad satires of generic choral groups or easy imitations of Muzak harmony won't go far. Though the class emphasizes quickness and alertness, we try to differentiate between a creative spontaneous response and a facile one. Some performance art composition is made thin by its easy cynicism. Some rock and roll is weighted down by its bloated passion. I emphasize a focus on detail, not on overall effect. Words are a helpful tool, even if the best composers turn out to be terrible lyricists.

A practical education should be a young composer's first priority. This part of your training acquaints you with all the possibilities that lie ahead and gives you the tools to realize what possibilities you choose to include in your musical domain. It gives you the skills you need to practice your craft. You are probably in no danger of forgetting that music is a holy and mysterious art. But it is just as important to remember Boulez's comparison of the composer to the plumber, whether you like his music or not.

FIVE

The Forms

Choosing the form that your music will take is a complex and highly subjective process. But there are some general guidelines to follow and questions to explore enroute to a decision. First, of course, it is important to be familiar with different forms, and you will most likely have gained this familiarity during your musical education. You will know what constitutes a symphony, a sonata, a string quartet, a concerto; that a motet is a polyphonic vocal composition, while a suite is a series of short movements, often dances, frequently preceded by a prelude. You will know the difference between a cantata and an oratorio. When you use dialogue conveyed via recitative, and arias, duets, quartets, and a chorus that gathers to praise, mourn, or thumb their noses at the characters and their actions, it is opera. When this kind of enterprise is cast in a so-called lighter vein (a distinction that has always seemed artificial to me), when the characters and the songs have a kinship with "popular" rather than "classical" music, it is operetta. Speak all the words and sing only songs, and you have vaudeville. Combine vaudeville with operetta, and musical comedy results.

This is barely a summary of different musical forms, and definitions change as new composers stretch their boundaries. The evolution of styles is painstakingly covered in music history classes, encyclopedias, and exhaustive studies written by everyone from Paul Hindemith, Aaron Copland, and George Martin to Philip Glass. I list styles because if a young composer is aware of rigid definitions and categories of classical, jazz, and pop music, she can better appreciate how the 1970s and 1980s mark an open season for creating new combinations of forms.

Electronic composer Morton Subotnick has composed a synthesizer/music theater piece for experimental vocalist Joan La Barbara. Mr. Subotnick is expanding his vision to encompass texts by Elie Wiesel and Virginia Woolf. Ms. La Barbara's voice and the synthesizer trade off and imitate each other. The composer wants to vary the usual concert experiences. The singer follows a complicated pattern of staging. There will be a set and props.

This is one illustration of how classical composers and performers are beginning to look for new ways to dramatize the concert form. David Bowie led a similar evolution in rock and roll with his Ziggy Stardust tour. "Crossover" is a common term today that characterizes certain artists of the musical world who have incorporated other than their usual techniques. Philip Glass, orginally considered a classical composer, has been heralded for bringing a new kind of music to rock audiences. The work resulting from his collaboration with Robert Wilson, *Einstein on the Beach*, combined electric music, Indian modes, and rock rhythms with Wilson's painterlike staging. Laurie Anderson used a fellowship from the National Endowment for the Arts to write a performance piece, "O Superman," which made the rock and roll charts and brought her a commercial record contract. Ms. Anderson combines classical/jazz violin with white rap, poetry, slides, and New Wave stand-up comedy. David Byrne crossed over from his Talking Heads rock and roll background to score films, and collaborate with Twyla Tharp on *The Catherine Wheel*. Stephen Sondheim worked against the linear form of the Broadway musical with *Sunday in the Park with George.* The first act is a visual collage that progresses toward a climax: the completion of a large painting by Seurat.

It seems that experimentation is more mainstream now than it's ever been. The composers I've mentioned are working professionals redefining the forms with which they've been struggling for years. They've won their right to be recognized; and their experimentation shouldn't be confused with more superficial eclecticism. Much of the video musical work on MTV, for instance, is facile and promotional. The visuals aren't connected to the audios, and their free associative quality is most often derivative—of Indiana Jones, *Flashdance,* Jordache commercials, or whatever is trendy. Abstract symbols suffer greatly when they're not informed by a knowledge of literature, musical culture, art, or politics. The lucky person who discovers an instantly successful way to express his musical vision is destined to repeat his formula. Still, the young composer is freer than ever to set aside notions of adhering to strict categories and to follow her own sounds.

But there are certain considerations you should be aware of as you seek to settle on a form for your music. Let's say you begin with some sounds in your head that combine in a melody. Would the melody lend itself best to instrumental treatment? Lots of instruments or a small group of perhaps just one? Should it be taken by a voice and accompanied by instruments? Is it a song? Should it have lyrics? If it's a song, are the instruments just backing it up or are they commenting? Perhaps four or five instruments are playing the piece. Does one take the lead, playing the melody in your head, while the other instruments talk around it? Do the instruments talk to each other or sing? What is the difference between talking and singing? If you're hearing something rhythmic, it's closer to talking. A smoother, legato line is related to singing. What instrument best suits the pitch of the sound you hear in your mind? What instrument is right for the energy, or impulse, of that sound? Is what you hear comic? Does it make you laugh? What instrument or voice corresponds to that laugh? If you're going to make a humorous world, who resides in it? Who moves around and who stays put?

As I've pointed out, in Ives' *Unanswered Question,* the voices of ancient wisdom move in major chords very, very slowly, and they barely change throughout the piece. When they do, it's as though the earth has heaved a great sigh. The trumpet that suddenly enters and asks its urgent question, sounds a little comic, even a little foolish. Then the flutes, with their high, perplexed voices, come in. The trumpet questions again, even more urgently. Eventually, all of Ives' winds come in, no one has any answers, and life goes on as it was before the question was asked. This work is a wonderful illustration of the distribution of energy and emotional content in a piece of music.

In a piece of yours, who stays? who goes? who gets excited? who remains calm? What kind of movements take place in your world of sound? Some sounds dart around more than others. Some appear briefly and are gone for a long time. Some appear, leave, and never return. Some change, some don't. The decisions you make about these matters lead you toward finding your form.

One form is more appropriate for certain sounds than another. Let's say the sun has come out for the first time in a week, there is a sharp wind blowing the sky clean of clouds, and I want to make a soundscape reflecting these circumstances. Do they constitute a symphony, 110 instruments celebrating the clouds rolling by? Not for me. The symphonic form would overwhelm such a delicate moment. Better to have just a flute and bassoon and let the bassoon drift off as the dark days depart, and the flute take over when the sunlight breaks. Another composer would disagree, hear the clouds as cellos, the clear sky as horns, the wind as chimes and oboes.

Subject matter dictates form. I am very stuck on words and drawn to forms that contain them rather than, say, to the symphony or the sonata. If I'm going to set an already existing text to music—something by Twain or Blake—the writer's voice will generally dictate the form. Blake's *Songs of Innocence and of Experience*, for example, had to be a suite. Each poem had to be a distinct entity. And even though the poems spoke of things that would be beyond a child's understanding, I heard the words sung in children's voices and set them that way.

When I approached the subject of the city of Jerusalem, a place filled with the sounds of many different voices, I had to ask myself some questions: did I want a plot, specific characters, with names, interacting with each other . . . Izzie goes to Jerusalem, meets Rachel, they move about the city, fall in love, settle down, etc? If so, I would have written an opera, operetta, or musical. But the voices I heard of Greek Orthodox priests, white and black Jews, Catholics, Armenians, Muslims, Moroccans, Turks, Ethiopian Coptics, were not specific people but elements of the great and turbulent city itself, an imagined, Felliniesque world of drift and disharmony. They were an oratorio.

In *The Beautiful Lady*, I wanted to set the poems of Anna Akhmatova, Marina Tsvetaeva, and Osip Mandelstam to music. As I read about their lives, I found out that they had been flamboyant adolescent geniuses hanging around a cabaret called the Stray Dog, which also attracted Pasternak, Meyerhold, and Mayakovski. The futurists, like our modern-day Beats, crashed poetry readings and acted out bizarre political protests. Their characters, the cabaret, and prerevolutionary St. Petersburg fascinated me. The poems became one small part of a more complex form. My wish to develop their characters and tell their life stories dictated the form of a musical. The nature of the Stray Dog Cabaret suggested a musical with a cabaret style and setting. The similarities between Dada, New Wave, and futurism inspired an experimental slant to my musical: presentational monologues and poetry readings as production numbers, narrative interrupting action, unexpected effects such as strong, dark, unidentifiable sounds to represent Akhmatova's "raven" or the coming revolution and its consequences.

Labels or comparison shouldn't stifle genuine enthusiasm and creativity in a young composer. Perhaps you decide to write a piece using many cellos. It might be discouraging for someone to say, "That's been done before, in the *Bachianas Brasileiras.*" Or someone responds to your use of many flutes playing at the same time by saying, "This is just like what Henry Brant did. What's new about it?" Or you're a young rocker, just getting your feet wet, and writing a short opera, maybe thirty minutes, that's confrontational and punk, and someone says, "You ought to listen to Brecht and Weill's *Little Mahagonny.*" There's nothing wrong with sharing musical impulses with distinguished predecessors. The creative problem is to go beyond being superficially derivative.

The composer writing for cellos should be aware of how Villa-Lobos wedded Bach with Brazilian folk music. She can hear the cellos and soprano vocalist create a mysterious, sensual quality. However, cellos can also be bullish, tragic, or comic. The number of cellos you choose is not the issue. Even if you wish to create a melodic melancholy like Villa-Lobos, if the melody is a strong sentence from your soul, your orchestration will respond to the intention, not the concept of numbers or instruments. The same is true for the short opera about a small town's decadence. Unless you intentionally steal from the libretto, or copy the German cabaret music hall style of Weill, you shouldn't be obsessed about your predecessors. I wasn't the first composer to set a

Greek tragedy to music. But I didn't think about precedent. I concerned myself with the passion and mystery behind the ancient languages I used as the basis for my vocal score. A composer who is intent on exposing the decadence of a small town may have gamblers and hookers as in *Mahagonny*, but if she follows the sounds and vocal patterns of her imaginary characters, she won't end up with a copy.

I have often used bird sounds in my work, and someone is always quick to remind me that Messiaen's music is rife with bird sounds. When I began in 1970 to put rap music in my songs, I was invariably told that it sounded like *Carmina Burana*. To me it sounded like Tibetan monks. There is nothing new under the musical sun. But these kinds of comparisons are beside the point and, if not educational, can be damaging. What is important is not what you are doing, but how you are doing it and why. Why do you make the choices you do? How does your particular voice speak through your music? What effect is that voice meant to have on your listeners?

Practical considerations also come into play when you are choosing a form. Maybe my impulse is to transform the day I described before—clouds giving way to sunshine— into a three-piano trio, one person playing in the bass, another playing bass and right hand, the third playing only right hand. That's fine, but if I don't have access to three pianos and/or three pianists, chances are good I won't hear my piece performed. Certainly, I can go ahead and write it anyway and hope that one day the pianos or the players will appear. On the other hand, I might decide to try it another way, with different instruments, ones I know will be available to me. When you're beginning your career, don't write a full, formal opera if you have no access to a cast who can sing it. Start with what you can hear performed. A painter limited to three colors will mix them together in different proportions until what he wants finally appears. By the same token, a composer should translate what exists inside her into the voices of two flutes, if that is what is available, or two bassoons, or a trumpet and a cello, or a tuba and French horn. Don't create something for a marching band unless you're willing to con the band leader into doing your piece and to hang out for a year in a high school.

While you are enduring these limitations (and you will), don't spend a lot of time lamenting the fact that you are being robbed of your dream. To exist as a composer you must give up some things in order to have other things come true. Such practical, workmanlike compromises can often lead to original, living music. Though I had planned to have five Ethiopian voices in *Jerusalem*, I ended up with one and had to alter my vision in a hurry. I used three black gospel singers to fill out the section. In six months of improvisation and composing, I developed combinations of sounds I'd never have discovered if I had stayed with the original concept. I juxtaposed "Amazing Grace" against an Ethiopian prayer song, and wrote a high-energy dance combining African, Mideastern, and up-tempo blues riffs. My music came out lively and real because I had to write for people discovering one another and delighting in one another's music.

The music I'm currently writing calls for a man who can play the piano, sing, and act, a combination I've never encountered in my life. I'm going to look for this person, but if I can't find him, I'll find another way to get the result I want. Guerrilla writing, invention that grows out of the materials you have at your disposal, tends to be organic and fresh. It comes from a true and fecund place inside you, not an intellectual one. A composer who is technically confident and improvisationally free will be able to respond to a challenge quickly and energetically. She will begin with specific solutions, but the whole self will inform the nuances. She will be like a good receiver catching an unexpected pass. The body and mind have mastered how to react. When you're in touch with a well-nurtured, spontaneous source of energy, you're less likely to make false or derivative choices.

Harold Pinter tells a story about a play he was writing. He imagined a house with his characters in it, and standing outside and longing to come in was another character, one Pinter found interesting, sometimes more so than the people inside. He says he knew he had to keep the door locked against this character because if he walked onstage the whole play would be ruined. A composer may experience a similar feeling when making a choice about lead instruments or melodic and rhythmic phrases. A sudden power element may tip the piece in a wrong direction, so it has to be sacrificed. Otherwise the composer must rethink the whole structure to feature the unexpected strong new force.

There is no *wrong* choice when settling on musical imagery and style. Different composers simply have different ways of looking at an event, and they express their points of view through metaphors of sounds. What if the episode involving the asthmatic Tuareg and me in the desert had fallen into George Gershwin's hands? I see a young woman in a skin-tight safari dress, the Tuareg in a matching khaki tie; when she comes upon him playing his flute, he throws it up in the air, catches a sax thrown him from the wings, plays a flashy solo, and then dances her over the dunes before they end up in the bar at the oasis, sharing a drink from a coconut with two straws. The music is lush and sexy, the pounding of Arabian horse hooves contrasts with the lonely solo of the lost American girl, she and the Tuareg fall in love, and maybe the romance will last, maybe it won't. It doesn't matter. As long as they dance.

Stravinksy would most likely have spurned both the linear structure and the story element. But he might have been fascinated by the subtle modulations of the wind as it fluttered through the Tuareg's indigo robe. His construction would represent layers of wind and sand, footsteps, desert silence, set against bursts of animal and human activity. He would have been concerned with temperature, humidity, shadow, light. His desert would be a mysterious, frightening place invaded by forces that collide, then back off.

Ives might take the same even and begin further back, hearing one of my fellow company members chewing gum as he climbs down from the Land Rover, another sucking on a tomato, a third humming while he cleaned his canteen. The crinkling tinfoil of a lunch being unwrapped, the flies buzzing around the lunch, would be in the music. Ives would calculate the mode of lunchtime conversation and the whistle of the wind. Eventually, he would pick up my lonely walk and the Tuareg's wheezing flute. He might have these sounds appear on and off at timed intervals, but he would also want them, at some point, to exist all at the same time. And, insofar as possible, he would want the instruments to sound exactly as rough, tired, scratchy, and annoying as the real thing.

And how would I—not being Gershwin, Stravinsky, or Ives—translate my Saharan encounter into a piece of music? If it were today, I would probably hand my ten-year-old lunch napkin, and a nose flute I picked up in the Agadès market, to a good ensemble player, a reed person with a jazz background, and ask him to give it a try. After we'd experimented with the instrument, I might ask him to wheeze a bit, too. I wouldn't ask him to re-create the mode, but rather to try to find the pattern that best evoked in the present the sense of loneliness, comedy, and peace that emanated from the Tuareg. Once we had the essence, I might take the player outdoors—to a rooftop, an outdoor theater, a balcony—to give a sense of space. At most, because I hear the piece as a solo, I would add percussion or vocal humming to supply the desert atmosphere. And the player would whisper in French. Play. Whisper. Play. Whisper. Wheeze. This reflects my point of view.

Is one of these versions, styles, forms, superior to another? I don't think so. Classical music, jazz, pop, ethnic music, hard-core rock, country-western, and show tunes have equal importance. Someone who writes rock and roll songs is no less a composer than one who writes string quartets. U2 would have transformed the moment into a driving tune using their Celtic rock style. The content might speak to the famine and sickness spreading in Africa, the message heightened by the force of the band. It would be just as valid as my rendition, or Gershwin's, or Stravinsky's. Any good composer utilizes his or her distinctive musical voice to make the present come to life. Whatever the form, the music relays a personal, urgent vision, and one can't help but listen.

What did I find compelling about the Tuareg's music? His mode was not particularly unusual. His asthma kept him from being a great player and caused his phrasing to jerk at untimely intervals. But in my naïveté, I probably imagined he was a devout Muslim and at peace with his surrounding and not afflicted with self-doubt. In my mind, he played his flute to keep himself company and to talk to God, so he really *spoke* through his phrasing. He seemed to appear, like an apparition, out of nowhere, speaking back to the wind as it howled at him. All these elements combined to make the moment unforgettable. But if I were to hear him every day, the novelty would wear off and so would my sense of wonder at his sounds. They would last longer if they were re-created, from a strong point of view, by Duke Ellington, or David Del Tredici, or Al Jarreau. This is the composer's job: to layer and orchestrate moments of music so that the final product creates, *every time,* the feeling of an event taking place for the first time.

When you choose a form, you must feel passionate

about its central ingredient, whether it be an instrument, a particular harmonic progression, and abstract sound, or a person or event you are commemorating or eulogizing. Form is shaped by your desire to pay the most expressive tribute you can to this element. How can you most eloquently speak, in a musical sense, of this element you love? What is the most striking sound painting you can make of it? As you address those questions, you define your form.

Perhaps the oboe is an instrument that thrills you. You love its sound and you want to write a piece of music that focuses on that sound. Ask yourself in what atmosphere you want your oboe to live: with a full orchestra cheering it on, or hanging out with a few friends, or in a conversation with one other voice? Or couch the questions in more dramatic terms: do you want the oboe in trouble (i.e., surrounded by turbulent strings), or on a quiet, solitary holiday, aggravated and provoked until it loses its temper?

While I was at Bennington, we received a flier from an organization that sought to strengthen the tuba repertoire by holding a tuba concerto–writing contest. I wanted to enter but didn't, and I've always regretted it. The tuba—that fat, sonorous, often gleeful, sometimes desolate instrument—strikes me as a powerful source of inspiration from the standpoint of either abstract sound or the concrete words it conjures. To me, tubas sound like hippopotamuses bathing in the river Niger.

Perhaps your animating passion is not an instrument but a particular interval; a minor third, for example C to E-flat, drums in your head like a repeated cowbell riff or a bird call. You love those intervals and want to celebrate them. That's fine. Any sound that excites you is worth saluting.

The problem is how to create a moving piece of music with minimal elements. Do you stay on the two notes and layer rhythmic variations on the patterns? Do you go off to a whole other melodic world and return to the original two notes? They say that Harold Arlen was stuck for a bridge for "Over the Rainbow." He kept searching for the notes that would connect the verses and move the drama forward. He finally found what he was looking for in the two notes he used when he whistled for his dog.

If you want to celebrate or memorialize a person, to write a musical love letter, in effect, think what form best represents that person—how can his or her internal workings be reflected in musical terms—and what kind of music would most please him or her. If I were to celebrate Henry Brant in music, for example, I would probably write something like a score for a Chaplinesque, Keystone Cops, wild silent movie. I'd alternate between atonal ragtime and honky-tonk, with humorous percussive crashes and twangs. In the midst of this musical melee, I'd insert a sweet, lyrical passage, romantic and dreamy and quintessentially American in its invocation of liberty, New England purity, and pride; then I'd go back to the madness. Henry Brant's music, his raincoat and baseball cap, fury and sweetness, is my personal point of departure. I know a young composer whose father was a respected musical theater composer. The son wanted to memorialize his father by weaving the letters of his name into a string sonata. He also found that he unconsciously began quoting themes from his father's shows.

You should bring to the decision about form the same kind of care, enthusiasm, and concentration you would expend on choosing a gift for your beloved. Members of my class do an exercise in which they write a piece of music about a scientific subject: electricity, gravity, energy, molecular movement, magnetic field. First they must study their chosen subject, and in doing so, they become involved with it, they grow to care about it, and this passion causes the subject matter and the musical form to fuse. You have to be in love with your subject when you choose a form.

Let's consider now in detail a few musical forms that utilize the human voice, and some of the challenges and pitfalls they present to a young composer. What might be the motivation, for instance, for writing an opera? It is not necessary to be sparked at the outset by a libretto or even a specific subject. Perhaps you simply want to use the human voice in a prominent and dramatic way, just as one might write a concerto for a revered instrument, drawn by a feeling of affection for it and a sense of all its possibilities. That's certainly reason enough. (Meredith Monk has often said her primary motivation for song writing is finding new sounds for the voice.) But if this is the case, beware of thinking that you are necessarily the person best qualified to pick the subject or supply the libretto. You may be. There are composers who manage to fill a dual role in the creation of an opera. But more often. I've seen such efforts founder because the composer insisted on being his own librettist.

What does one look for in a libretto? The trend up until now has certainly not been complex writing. There is even an argument to be made that simple words better serve the broad drama presented in conventional opera. Someone who is seeking a librettist should look for a gifted writer who also understands the needs of music. The collaborations of Virgil Thomson and Gertrude Stein were early efforts at allowing experimental literature to participate in the music. Look for a writer who is literate, who has worked in other media, and whose gift allows his or her work to stand on its own. Look for someone who has a sense of metaphor, of character, of speech and its rhythms, of dramatic development. The text of a libretto should have its own integrity and speak to the problems, hopes, and choices of the characters, just as good contemporary fiction does. Its subject matter may be grounded in the past, but its voice should be contemporary.

How rare are the operatic characters who speak to our time. Are we somehow undeserving of embodiment in the operatic form because we no longer die of consumption, because our problems are more internalized and our emotions less flamboyant? Of course not. There are contemporary stories every bit as appropriate for operatic treatment as the grandiloquent tales of the past: stories of women struggling against historical impediments, of men and women trying more honestly to understand each other, of children finding their way in a dislocated world, of people trying to stay alive on the streets of the cities and on the farms in the countryside, of people dealing with corrupt government and the poisoned environment. It is bizarre that the New York City Opera's premiere of *Malcolm* (based on the life of Malcom X) was considered such an unusual event. The main reason is that the better-known opera companies are only beginning to open their repertoires to contemporary librettos and nonlinear forms. Perhaps this is why some modern composers have named their modern operas performance art, dance cycles, music theater. Terry Riley, Laurie Anderson, Carla Bley, Philip Glass, and others are breaking poetry up into soundscores or returning to ancient languages—Sanskrit, Latin, classical Greek—and focusing on languages as music as well as literal speech.

In these contemporary works, the language in effect is part of the music, and listening to it is in some ways like listening to a symphonic concert. The human voice, however, always brings with it certain unique and private intonations and emotions, and these invariably come through, even though the sounds are not familiar to the Western ear. Experiencing this, the audience is bound to change its conception of what emotion is. They are not hearing Western sadness, or jubilation, or rage. Nor is it Eastern, Asian, African. There is no automatic associative reference point. And when this works, it is stunning and exciting in a way that nothing else is. I have occasionally been transported by my own efforts in this regard. I have also been humiliated and reduced to helpless laughter when it hasn't worked and has come out sounding like elevated baby talk.

This raises an issue that must be considered by the opera composer. Whom are you writing for? If it's for a Western, classical operatic voice, don't use Ethiopian Coptic, Armenian, Sanskrit, or any other language that requires a combination of chest voice, head voice, resonators, or Tibetan, African, or Indian singing techniques. One had only to witness the New York City Opera's production of Philip Glass's *Akhnaten* to know how disastrous such a mismatch can be. Singers must be trained to produce the sounds of ancient languages. Otherwise you end up with babble.

One way to deal with this is to build your company, collecting, auditioning, and training the voices over the years with specific work in mind. I've done this often, working as long as a year with a group of people to get them to sing the way I want for a particular piece. This is rather like making an instrument for a specific concert, and it can be extremely satisfying. When the New York City Opera considered *Jerusalem*, Beverly Sills, the company's manager, came to hear a run-through. She listened, liked it, and, when it was over, turned to me and said, "How in the world can my people do it? And why have them try to imitate these voices when these voices do it so well?" She was right, of course.

The more likely scenario for a young opera composer is that she will be invited to work with an existing opera company. Should this occur, do not be a snob and demur and say you can only work with people of your own choosing. Recognize that you will be dealing solely with operatic, Western, classical voices, and write accordingly. Wonderful things can be done with operatic voices, and when they are effective, they are so musical, so well trained, so athletic, that the voice itself incorporates an emotion that all the bad acting in the world can't destroy.

Until recently, I've had little use for the European-derived, stylized form of trained singing. In this genre, the voice itself always seemed artificial to me. The sounds that classical singers produce do not go directly to my heart, but rather to my head first, and then my feelings slowly catch up. The sense of distance this creates, however, can be put to good dramatic use. And were I to find myself writing for a company of such voices, I would decide which concepts of mine were appropriate for them, which were not. I would also, most likely, ask myself what other kind of singers I could add to the company, perhaps recruiting some kids from local schools, maybe adding a rock performer or two. I would do this for the same reason another composer chooses a flute, oboe, and synthesizer for a score. I would want to vary and modernize my vocal orchestration. Perhaps there would be resistance at first, but eventually the opera singers and popular singers would benefit from each other's experience.

Rock and roll is the most important new musical environment of the last thirty years, and it is, in its own way, as broad, as extreme, and as loud as grand opera. The term "rock opera" has been misapplied to such works as *Hair, Tommy, Sgt. Pepper,* and *Jesus Christ Superstar.* The last comes closest, perhaps, but it's really something between light opera and musical theater with a bit of a rock beat and superficial character songs. Basically, it's easy-listening pop with good lyrics. And the mind behind it, Andrew Lloyd Webber's, is essentially commercial. A genuine rock opera, something that captures the passionate, fiery, rhythmic elements of that enraged art form, with a plot and characters that combine in a theatrical form, has not yet been written. And rock's confessional nature, though fine in itself, is a real stumbling block toward writing workable dramatic songs.

Nowhere is this displayed more vividly that on MTV. There are some encouraging aspects to the musical video scene. The incorporation of difficult dance into musical numbers is beginning to interest young people in the art of dance, and I'm grateful for that because dance is an essential part of musical theater. Also, artists who could easily limit themselves to making records are attempting to explore the visual world. Unfortunately, their sense of imagery is mostly based on a kind of mindless free association, and the result typically is somewhere between a Michelob commercial and a soft-core porno film. But the main problem, the built-in limitation, is the nature of the rock song.

A dramatic song is organically connected to the individuality of the character who sings it. The urgent "I" and "he" or "she" in rock are usually a standardized self and other in a situation of pleasure and/or pain, and whatever narrative there is gets dropped for the duration of a chorus in which everyone joins. Exceptions are the story songs of Simon and Garfunkel and Bruce Springsteen and the political songs of writers like Phil Ochs, Randy Newman, and Suzanne Vega, whose subjects are more broadly based. Their point of view however, is still internal.

Because such songs are written to be complete in themselves, they leave nothing to be developed and usually pull out all the stops for an emotional build. For instance, "White Rabbit," the Jefferson Airplane's hit song, tells a story about drugs. It's a powerful hallucinatory song evoking *Alice in Wonderland* and creates a terrifying electrified mood. Similarly, "I Need a New Drug" by Huey Lewis says all it needs to say about the subject and the singer. And in many cases, the idiosyncratic style of the singer is what the song is really about. Grace Slick and Michael Jackson aren't characters in a drama, they are figures in rock culture. As long as rock and roll centers around the persona of the lead singer, musicals in this genre will be hard to create. Also, in rock, music and lyrics become one, and the persuasive beat makes you want to get up and dance. The very elements that create good rock make bad theater. You should not want to get up and dance with a character who is not even supposed to know you're there.

Furthermore, the joy of noise that I mentioned before is a crucial element of rock feeling. This often eliminates the need for precisely understanding lyrics. The catching of an occasional word, picking up the gist of a chorus hook, is the first experience of a rock tune, which, like a good poem, is designed to reveal other levels only after several hearings. I love this aspect of rock, and spent many hours of my adolescence listening over and over to *Sgt. Pepper's Lonely Hearts Club Band*, "Mass" by the Electric Prunes, and Otis Redding's tunes, but as a theater musician I know that songs written to be complete in themselves can't develop a narrative, character, or theme. It's a tribute to the supreme gifts of Cole Porter, Rodgers and Hart, Leonard Bernstein, and other theater composers that they stayed true to a story's dramatic needs and still produced song standards. One of the primary reasons why so few Broadway musicals make it to the mainstream is their failure to address the current music of the masses—which is rock and roll. A song like "Memory" from *Cats,* in which the creators of the show simply abandoned T. S. Eliot's text and wrote catchy lyrics, is an obvious pitch for commercial success. They got their pop feel even if it meant abandoning the show's most vital muse. Most musicals that try to incorporate rock or pop seem destined, up to this date, for mushy, synthesized hybrid scores or plotless, nostalgic collages. *Beatlemania* and *Leader of the Pack* had great singers but nonexistent books and arbitrary staging. *Tommy* did not become a movie without sacrificing the vitality of its score.

The lack of story is also evident in most video products, and that undercuts their possibilities as a dramatic breeding ground. Certainly a story needn't unfold in A, B, C, D order. The Talmud says that we can tell a story in any order we like. This implies that the definition of "story" is found in the telling. But often music videos have no story at all, or they have a vague story and quickly opt out of it in order to chase after some disconnected images.

To be sure, rock has shown little interest in adapting to dramatic forms. But given its angry energy and its desire to speak out, rock might well find an interesting partner in a theatrical form in which character is central and there is an inner and outer world to be explored. I urge my students, particularly the few who know, say, Chekhov and Shakespeare as well as rock music, to attempt such a union. And maybe one or another of them will be able to bring it off. I hope so. I'd like to hear and see it.

Musical theater is a form I want to examine in depth, not only because it is my area of greatest experience, but because music is innately theatrical, and the infusion of theatrical ideas and principles can vitalize any kind of music. Also, it provides an apt focus for what is effective and ineffective in other forms of music. Its basic values apply to most modes of human expression. At this point in history, musical theater for the most part is not any more dynamic or relevant or eloquent than conventional opera, whose liabilities I've just described. It is another musical form in need of massive transfusions of new blood.

We are familiar with the old-fashioned musical. It opens with a rousing production number to catch 'em; follows up with a number to catch 'em and hook 'em; continues with a ballad that most likely introduces the longings of the hero and heroine to move 'em; then moves steadily toward the climax of the first act, which is an up-tempo number to grab 'em before intermission. Usually third from the end is the eleven o'clock number, the single that will sell the show, the confessional, heartrending, turn-the-character-around ballad. And of course the show must end with another stirring production number.

This formula has worked well in the past and can still be made effective by catering to the audience's nostalgic impulses. But while this is satisfying to someone seeking to be soothed by the sounds of the past, it is death to the form itself. Hence it is necessary to concoct ever more elaborate methods of manipulation to keep the audience's attention and sustain the illusion that the form is still alive.

Shows like *A Chorus Line* or *Cats* or *Sweeney Todd* manage through ingenious reinvention to fool us into thinking they are revolutionary variations on the musical comedy form. But they are really gutsy blood cousins of the formulaic musical, and they offer the same razzmatazz and entertainment values. *Hair*, which "revolutionized" theater for about a year, and which had a brilliant score, was really an imaginatively organized sixties happening put on the stage for a bourgeois audience. It did not break any ground that pointed toward a redefinition of the form. There is a place for shows like these in our musical life, just as there is a place for conventional grand opera, but what will revitalize the life of the musical theater? I teach a course called "Alternatives to Musical Theater." At the outset, I invite the students to disagree with me and to demonstrate that the standard form is still a viable one.

The American musical was conceived for a historical time quite different from the present. The popular culture of the 1930s and the 1940s and early 1950s was a relatively naive, idealistic, and romantic one (though the times themselves were brutal). The characters in musicals, with a few exceptions like Rose in *Gypsy*, had an aura of innocent "Aw, shucks," about them, and their conflicts and resolution were simplistic. Think of *Oklahoma!*, *Carousel*, *The King and I*, *Pal Joey*, and *Guys and Dolls*. Today, in a society that has come a long way from "Aw, shucks," writers don't believe the simplicities and clichés of their conventions, the audience knows instinctively it's being handed something bogus, and so more money, more elaborate gimmicks, more spectacular costumes, and flashier orchestrations are required to cover up the essential emptiness of the undertaking. When one feels uncomfortable in the theater, it is almost always because something is phony. Something genuine, whatever its drawbacks, doesn't make us squirm. Lotte Lenya was never touted for her dulcet singing voice, but when she performed Kurt Weill's music, few doubted the credibility of her performance.

Unquestionably, the 1980s are obsessed with style rather than content. We are in a director's era. Even the avant-garde, which thinks it is addressing content, is simply caught up in the style of the content. The questions people ask about avant-garde work are decidedly style oriented. "Is it musical theater? Is is poetic theater? Is it dance or drama? Is it ritualistic?" Better they should ask: "Is it any good? Is it dramatic? Does it move you?" Robert Wilson's highly stylized, dreamlike theater with Philip Glass' musical accompaniment is beautiful, but it is extremely arcane and European and has no relation to the dying form of America's sincere, good-natured musical comedy. He shouldn't be called a revolutionary in American musical theater, because there is very little that is American in either Glass' music or Wilson's visual styles. David Byrne's collaboration with Twyla Tharp in *The Catherine Wheel* used song and dance in new ways, but created too abstract a world to be compared with musical theater. Martha Clarke's *Garden of Earthly Delights* is another work acclaimed for its innovative musical theatrical style. The piece uses one of the most talented theatrical composers, Richard Peaslee, but there are no songs, and the emphasis on movement seems to make this and *The Catherine Wheel* experiments in dance, not musical theater. Laurie Anderson creates a full multimedia, words-music-movement experience. Her epic *U.S.A.* might have been called musical theater, as might Tom Waits' gritty, staged Broadway show. But music and movement centering around one person is still performance, and though innovative, these two artists can only feed what must be ultimately a bigger form if we are to mix the old and the new, and come up with musical *shows*.

Another complication in the demise of the musical is the extreme fragmentation that exists in the musical world. In pre–World War II America, and for a time after the war as well, the popular music of the day was similar to show music. The music of Rodgers and Hammerstein and Rodgers and Hart and Jerome Kern sounded like the music one heard on the radio. Clearly, that is not so today. Popular music is dominated by the youth culture, by the sensibility reflected in hard and soft rock, rhythm and blues, country-western. But very little of this is reflected in musical theater, or in any other dramatic vocal art form, for that matter. Also, today each audience member and composer is a specialist of sorts—a rock expert, country-western expert, classical expert, jazz expert—and there is little educated combining of these different factions in any audience or composer except in the most rarified progressive circles.

One might think the string of highly successful musicals based on black performers and writers are an exception. *Ain't Misbehavin'*, *Eubie!*, *Bubbling Brown Sugar*, *Mama, I Want to Sing*, and *Dreamgirls* have flourished with all kinds of audiences. The arrangements are tight; the performances have energy equal to that of rock and roll, and the music and lyrics are sometimes intelligent and resonant. However, if you examine these shows closely, you'll realize that they are mostly reviews of old-time jazz composers, and the content is nostaligc, comforting, familiar. In the case of *Mama, I Want to Sing*, you have a book that barely strings together phenomenal performances of traditional gospel. *Bubbling Brown Sugar*'s book defers to old-time music hall performances. *Dreamgirls* has original music, but it purposely derives from styles of the Supremes, Temptations, and Four Tops because Michael Bennett wanted to trace the rise of a singing group like the Supremes from anonymous poverty to superstardom.

These are basically all *concept* shows, which give great performers a chance to show their stuff. A concept show has a simple, straightforward, marketable theme. One can almost plan the merchandising before the script is finished. Content remains nostalgic and safe, therefore audiences across the board can find entertainment. Even an experimental version of the black musical, Lee Breuer's *Gospel at Colonus*, is an entertaining transposition of the Oedipus myth performed by old-time gospel groups, huge choirs, and great black soloists. In the case of *Dreamgirls* and *The Gospel at Colonus*, both the concepts and music were created by whites. I'm not disparaging the fine moments these pieces brought to their audiences, and I am particularly grateful for the performance values but, as I ask my students, what are slick reviews of jazz standards gospel, and imitation Motown doing for the forms of musical theater? It seems to me that Broadway is moving backward, and the music being written (or ar ranged) for Broadway is standing still. The popularity of nostalgia raises disturbing political questions a young composer ought to be aware of. Music can't change political trends, but it ought to be a strong provocative force. The lack of real political risk in any mainstream musical piece is a terrible indictment of the theater.

Can any kind of music bridge such deep and definite gaps? Can musical theater capture any part of the tone of this decade? Tackling these questions in class, we usually arrive at the conclusion that we want to discard the current categories of style, refusing to be bound by them just because critics and theorists are, and to focus instead on what works, what brings a reality onstage that sings and moves and resonates. The focus of the course becomes the effort to compose a lively, unpretentious, genuine piece of theatrical music.

The form the music takes is dictated by the diverse personalities and tastes of the students in the class. It might be a tap dance or a soft-shoe number, hard-core rock or an aggressive slam dance, a country tune with a soft rock beat or a classically inspired "show tune." It doesn't really matter. What matters is the passion that has motivated the creator, passion for the thing itself, not because it will please an audience, make back an economic investment, satisfy a label, or garner press attention.

To begin to innovate, we clearly must move beyond the structural confines of the "book" musical. And we can once again find clues in the recent experiments of Martha Clarke and Dick Peaslee, Richard Foreman and Stanley Silverman, Stephen Sondheim and James Lapine. All have tried valiantly, but have fallen short of making a new and lasting form. In a concert version of *Alice* with Meryl Streep that I did at the Public Theater some years ago, I placed the characters on stage in chairs, and Ms. Streep sat on the floor. The characters came together whenever a scene called for it, there was dancing and movement but no set, and each character had a distinct musical signature: the Caterpillar was an Indiana raga, the Duchess was a samba, the Red Queen was a vicious tango, Humpty-Dumpty had an oom-pah feeling. I remember thinking at the time, "Remember this, it's the beginning of a new form and you should hang on to it." Later, we did a more elaborate version of *Alice* with sets and staging, and I succumbed to pressures for a stronger "book" and bigger production. The pretty lights and dances were all well and good, but in giving up my original vision, I lost the real spark. The second *Alice* didn't work nearly as well.

It is passion more than any arbitrary form or charismatic star that will resuscitate the musical theater. Its world is a fascinating and artificial one in which people express their emotional life in song and we believe them. In the course of daily life, people having marital spats, walking down the street discussing politics, complaining about their knee joints, or celebrating a lottery win do not break into metered rhythm with perfect melodies that resolve into a major chord break. Nor does a group of people at a bullfight, a dinner party, or a bar mitzvah, whether it is happy or sad or angry, burst into a chorus that ends up with Handel-like antiphonal voices and all hands rising into the air simultaneously. This musical theater convention is obviously to real life what the Marx Brothers are to a nice, normal young man.

But there can be something beautiful and significant in this unreality. In a world governed by theater time, events are magically heightened and distilled. They occur in a space that is initially empty, and that gradually fills with voices making it lively and resonant. Light enters the space, bodies within it begin to move in rhythm, and the life that exists in the space for a given period of time is more vivid and compelling than any other life we know. The music in this world, the songs, are messengers from an acute and heightened part of the human consciousness. You can hear it in the older musicals when, in its right time and place, a show tune stepped out from the action of its story and sang to everyone. *Showboat, West Side Story, Gypsy,* or *Lady in the Dark* may seem hackneyed now, but their songs had an electrifying effect on the era in which they came into being. Single songs like "Ol' Man River" could even produce new consciousness in its audience. Later on, Dick Peaslee and Peter Brook created a shocking musical asylum in *Marat/Sade,* which defined much of the artistic climate of the sixties, particularly after Judy Collins recorded the themes and popularized them.

But as we've moved into the seventies and eighties, single songs have become souvenirs from incomplete works. "Send in the Clowns" is perhaps the most touching song left over from an unsuccessful show by Stephen Sondheim. "Ease on Down the Road" from *The Wiz* is another case of a show being saved by a song. It got covered and was played on the radio, and audiences flocked to hear the rest of the score, which was full of effects and momentarily pleased them but left little resonance. I've spoken of the good business sense of putting "Memory" in *Cats*. Audiences responded to the raw intensity of Jennifer Holliday's performance at the end of act 1 in *Dreamgirls*. There is no denying that millions of people were moved by the image Michael Bennett gave us of the line of courageous survivors in *A Chorus Line*. However, they are fragments, and particularly in the last fifteen years, we seem to depend on and be satisfied with such fragments. No contemporary composer has yet produced a whole evening as informed and empowered as a night with an inspired, contemporary stand-up comic or rock group. Commercial success may require confidence, skill, and luck, but these elements alone don't suffice to create real theater, the kind that is rooted on ritual and draws its inspiration from the needs and faith of its community.

When you attend a church or synagogue or mosque to listen to its music, you feel the weight of its history, its sense of mystery, the darkness and the light, the fear and exaltation that lives within it. Its songs are like old stories, passed on through families and teachers. The effect of such music is deep, the way a loved one can evoke an emotion that no stranger can. That is the power of theater.

Most children have the experience of watching their parents become different people in certain situations, for example at the dinner table, at work, and at a party. So they learn that people wear masks that turn them into other people, that they take on different voices and manners, that they even long to be someone else. The human need to "act" is theater.

Because music has an ability to convey emotion that even eloquent speech lacks, musical theater has a dimension that straight theater does not. A song, if it is well done, is written in the voice, key, and rhythm of the character who sings it. It not only reflects the character—song and person become one and the same. Also, the music and lyrics become one, the lyrics themselves taking on a kind of rhythm, becoming another kind of sound. Think of *The King and I*. The king's choppy rhythm and peculiar voice aid in the creation of this brusque character from a strange culture. The somewhat fussy music sung in the beginning by the formal British schoolteacher Anna becomes more fluid and lyrical as she softens. Think of the strippers' number in *Gypsy*: "You can pull all the stops out, / till they call the cops out." It's a wonderfully lively presentation of strippers, cheerful in its outlook, instructive in its message, redolent of vaudeville, and yet it has its own distinct identity, as does the voice of each of the strippers singing it. This is very good musical writing: character transmutes into music, the music is one with the character.

By the same token, it is a mistake in musical theater to saddle a character with the author's message. Stephen Sondheim is guilty of this in some of the numbers in *Company* and *Follies*, in which he takes society to task and bemoans the prevalence of compromise and selling out. His sentiments are justified, but his characters can't hold their own opinions and his as well. Brecht and Weill managed to create a distanced style where characters become ideas and forces in themselves, and Brecht made no attempt to endow his characters with naturalistic human needs. The political commentary shaped his tone, and therefore his songs didn't compromise.

In my show *Runaways,* I made the same mistake Sondheim did. The show is essentially a rock-salsa-rap ritual to help those children who are the victims of parental abuse and social neglect. This "message," for the most part, is carried in songs that accord with the characters played by the kids. Because the music is wedded to character, the show is not filled with protest songs. However, in the second act, there is a song with a kind of reggae beat called "We Are Not Strangers." The words to the chorus are:

> Blow thin wind
> across the pine
> We have a fire
> to warm cold hands
> Dusty boots—
> now rest a while
> We are not strangers
> We are not strangers
> We are not strangers
> In fact I know you well.

It's a nice song (as are the Sondheim tunes I alluded to), and performed by itself, it's effective as a piece of music. As part of the show, however, it's a dud because its broadly optimistic tone does not gibe with the language or tone of any of the specific kids. They are not singing it. *I* am. I was more concerned, in this instance, with the idea I was trying to convey—the concept of sisterhood and brotherhood among the lost children of the world—than I was with character. And in musical theater, that is always a mistake. An idea cannot have emotion. An idea cannot change as a result of experience. An idea cannot travel from one place to another within a play. Only a character can do that. More often than not, this kind of mistake can be traced to the business mentality of the composer, the ambitious part that wants a hit song as well as an effective one.

I hasten to add that you needn't limit your idea of character to a three-dimensional person in a sailor suit on the deck of a yacht. A character needn't even be human. It can be anything as long as it has an active emotional life. The Bread and Puppet Theater has succeeded in creating music for spirits, monsters, planets, and trees; puppetry teaches performers how the inanimate can be endowed with spiritual life.

As a composer for the musical theater, you must pay close attention to your inner life and to other people in order to develop a thorough understanding of human emotion. You must also know precisely what emotion you want to convey. You would be surprised how often a student attempts to capture an event without knowing why the moment was so attractive, what the players were really feeling. At the same time, do not be seduced into thinking that one of your emotional/musical impulses necessarily constitutes the basis for a musical. If you feel, for instance, like writing a powerful, unrestrained, tragic wail, don't rush to create an arbitrary context for it, to tack on a story that will justify fulfilling this urge. Discard temporarily the notion of a musical, and write a dirge or a requiem instead. Before embarking on a musical, make sure the characters are present in your mind and even walking around in it.

To carry this admonition one step further, do not build a musical around the theme of a hit song (*Evita* seems wound around variations of "Don't Cry for Me, Argentina"). If your motivation is to come away with a "property," you are in trouble. A musical should not be a "vehicle" for anything: a song, a dance, a dancer, a singer. Some of Kander and Ebb's work since *Cabaret* seemed built around specific star performers. Once this happens, you're not thinking about characters and their emotional life. You are thinking about the actors for whom you're writing and, most likely, recapitulating and reinforcing his or her performance clichés. That's not fair to the actor, and it's not good for your work.

This is not to say that you should never write anything with a particular performer in mind. A healthy collaborative relationship shouldn't be confused with a commercial package. Before beginning rehearsals of the production of *Alice*, I told Meryl Streep the music was written and asked if there was something she would like included. She said she would love a song that sounded like Purcell. I wrote a tune in that vein about how wonderful the world feels to a little girl, how it seems that she owns everything, and everything is at her command. Ms. Streep's request was a good inspiration for me. But if I had known that she was going to play Alice when I was writing the rest of the show, I might have censored my instincts to be playful and nasty in deference to her dignified, intelligent persona. As it is, we both benefited.

"Hey, let's write a break-dancing musical!" is not a good starting point, either. What is the passion behind such an enterprise? What's the story? The reason for its existence? Because break dancing looks good on video? Because it sells sneakers? Examine your motives scrupulously and ask yourself some hard questions before getting carried away by your own impulses. A composer I know once wanted to do a show that had two pianos, one a man, one a woman, interacting with each other. It's a perfectly nice idea, but for a piano duet, not a musical, and the musical failed.

Once you have decided that your idea is suited to the musical form, and you have your story and your characters, let the characters tell you what emotions to express, and be certain that those emotions are intelligent. Any emotion, if it is true, is intelligent. Even a stupid character can express intelligent emotion. But you must know the difference.

Because if you think emotion itself is stupid, rest assured you will write a stupid song.

What is intelligent emotion? In a typical musical, a grieving woman sings about a lover who is going off to war. The distraught woman sings heavy music that feels like "Oh, what if I lose this wonderful man, he was just what I wanted, all that I dreamed of, but now he is going, I will wait by the window," etc. This is unintelligent emotion because it tells you nothing about human desire and fear. It is melodramatic, generalized. Instead of speaking to our imagination, it merely invokes the clichés of second-rate operas and bad acting classes.

Now consider the moment in Peter Brook's *King Lear* when Paul Scofield, as Lear, discovers Cordelia dead. He utters a single cry that is terrifying and poignant. It depicts madness and grief. The two pitches of this cry are full and resonant, and so specific they could be notated. Scofield's voice is full of vibrato, rasp, and gentleness, so musical that his sounds are not accidental or improvisational, though inspired by the drama of the moment. He and Brook created a song for that heartbreaking moment of loss, and it is committed, precise, and yet intelligent because of all it seems to convey. Scofield's cry is the root of an intelligent, musical song. Any composer aspiring to write dramatically should know the difference between this true emotional moment and phony melodrama. Music is a recapitulation of emotion. The controlled distance music creates between the listener and the situation that gives rise to it helps us to take fuller account of our own emotions than we normally do.

True emotion is visceral and unconcerned with displaying itself. It does not preen, it lacks self-consciousness, and it comes from a spontaneous place within us. When it is censored, maimed or manipulated, the result is the artifice and pretense of most TV shows and many films.

Musical theater at its best, with dance and song and harmony and instrumental music and acting and lively characters who have been created and developed imaginatively, is for me the most magical use to which music can be put. It has everything I can imagine wanting. I think back to my parents' love of Rodgers and Hammerstein's shows of the fifties, how they rhapsodized about the wartime musicals. When I see revivals of *The King and I, Oklahoma!, State Fair,* and *Carousel,* I am moved by the lush orchestrations and generous choreography. I understand how the naïveté and buoyancy of such shows soothed the spirits of a country traumatized by a world war but full of romantic patriotism.

When I've watched ritual masquerades in Nigeria or witnessed the samba parades in Brazil, I've seen a musical theater that invokes and speaks to the spirit of a whole village. A similar enactment of our more sophisticated and diffuse culture in a musical that speaks to one or more of the issues of our time, whose energy activates our deadened spirits, is what I long for and work for. Surely the amazing advances in media haven't deprived our senses and emotions of experiencing wonder from a live story with expressive songs and dances. At the same time, it is true that today's theater audience is different from that of thirty years ago. Overstimulated and saturated by the stunning tricks that technology can perform, the audience expects musical theater to provide more of the same. We are besieged with the likes of singers in furry body stockings levitating while singing ballads, and revolving stages supporting choruses of armored robots on roller skates. But a young composer shouldn't confuse spectacle with passion, shouldn't be afraid to confront the issues of our time and express his or her opinions through living characters and ideas. The old musical theater delighted its innocent audiences with orchestral overtures, tap dances, and romantic interludes. Today's composers face a more wary and benumbed population. But surely musical theater is still capable of the energy and relevance it has had in the past, and when contemporary forms are found for it, the theater will be as exciting and as liberating as it used to be.

SIX

Rewriting

MOZART SUPPOSEDLY WROTE many of his works in one draft. It's nice to think that composers are vessels for divine spirits, and that inspiration can be absolute, but unfortunately the reality for most composers is that they must be willing to rewrite their music. "Talent" also means the ability to solve the problems that any creative process brings upon itself.

Learning to rewrite means first acknowledging that something is wrong. A young composer can be so amazed that she has actually finished a piece of work that the recognition of its flaws is intolerable. But if you have a sense of humor about yourself and a resilient ego, you'll soon learn that the beginnings of real musical growth lie in addressing your lazy, facile, or excessive writing.

The first step is to search for weaknesses. After an initial proud, loving internal performance of your score, listen again. (You can listen to the written score in your head, ask friends to play it for you, duplicate sounds on a synthesizer, or overdub your own playing on a four-track Portastudio.) There are several ways to listen for problematic writing. One way is free-floating concentration. You simply listen without any goal in mind. As you listen, you ask yourself if the overall effect is what you intended. Is the general energy less than you thought? Why are you left with the memory of an instrument you didn't intend to feature? Do you feel distracted during some sections? Do your builds go as high as you imagined, your quiet sections hush the atmosphere in the way you thought they would? Is your emotional intent clear? Are the rhythms and accents as lively and shocking as you hoped?

A general, elusive problem usually points to some very specific solutions. Last year I wrote a movie theme that I'd intended to be dark and somewhat disturbing, but more of a premonition than a flat-out emotional statement. When I heard the theme played, I was horrified to hear that although it started out correctly, it became maudlin, overbearing, and then sort of like a Hungarian version of the theme from *Jaws*. I listened to it again to try to understand what I'd done wrong. In the first place, I'd written the second half of the theme too low for a cello, so that it sounded thick and sentimental. Second, I had all the strings bowing in triads, so the orchestration sounded romantic, mushy, and without any edge. Last of all, I'd given too many low instruments important lines. The alto flute, string bass, low register on English horn, and timpani all doubled the main theme. This wasn't a premonition of dying, but a prolonged death.

My next listen was inside my head. I systematically analyzed the problems and used my technical expertise to change the tone. I kept most of the main theme, but took out one interval that was too tragic. I kept the cello, but transposed several sections up an octave, and asked the player to hit each note with less intensity and let up on the vibrato during sustained tones. I asked the other string players to play the written notes but in unison and pizzicato. This took away the unintentional sentimental string pad. I cut the English horn, told the timpanist to begin his part thirty-two measures later in the orchestration, and wrote a new part for the alto flute that was less busy and contained sparse, repeated "calls." I rewrote the contrabass line and had him pluck harmonics. This course of action was a simple rewrite. My theme needed a small revision. I weeded the thick orchestration; I redistributed the bottom-heavy lines and found a new, breathier timbre. When I was finished, the theme worked.

Sometimes this kind of drastic last-minute work can be avoided by a ruthlessly objective checklist on the first listen. Each composer will have his own. Mine would be: Can every instrument be heard? Is there any instrument that sounds out of place playing the lines it's been assigned? Is any section too crowded, too sparse? Am I reaching dynamic peaks too soon? Am I drowning out the melodic line with my choice of harmony? Are too many instruments playing lead lines? Are sections with different orchestral textures in the right proportion to each other? Is a pattern repeating itself too much? Too little? Have I voiced the leading line too high for its intention? Am I losing resonance and clarity in the lower registers of my instruments? Are my melodic variations too intricate, simplistic?

These questions are applicable to any style of music. A symphony can suffer from an overabundance of heavy string lines; a rock song can fall apart under a hysterical lead guitar line; a piano sonata can lose clarity because of crowded, busy collisions between the hands; the words of a vocal quartet can be indecipherable because too many lines move simultaneously; a percussion piece can lose its momentum by becoming too spare, too fast; a harmony's intrinsic beauty can be sacrificed because it comes in and out for arbitrary reasons. A composer in any genre has to have a strong sense of why sound is placed where it is whether his choices are motivated by instinct or rules.

I've never believed explanations by composers such as "I don't know why it works; it just does." Often a composer doesn't know why a moment works while she is discovering it, but she has to have developed a vocabulary to identify and convey successful effects, even if it's as eccentric as Thelonious Monk's strange tap dances during rehearsals of his tunes. Rather than play, he listened to his band by dancing against the music.

Often the first draft of a musical composition will not be as moving, scary, heartbreaking, or fiery as you want. It's hard to locate the mistake in a piece that fails on an emotional level. Music that might not seem sad or reverent enough to its composer has to be analyzed for its technical deficiencies. Rarely does a successful rewrite come from working on becoming more inspired or profound. That's just too general a place to start.

I'd recommend that before embarking on a soul-searching quest, the young composer start with practical questions. Is the piece too long? Have you taken a valid emotional impulse and simply overstated it? For instance, the "Jewish Quarter" of *Jerusalem* is a musical collage based on a series of loving, happy prayers, dances, and stories repeatedly interrupted by shocking, violent sounds. The percussive interruptions are meant to express the fear of the memory of annihilation and are always followed by guttural, sustained wails of grief. A prayer changes to a festive song, and this to a strident explosion that settles into a lament. Each progression proved to be very effective. The idea of repeating this kind of cycle was appealing to me. I decided to repeat it four times. However, when I ran the "Jewish Quarter" as a whole, it seemed sluggish. The music was mushy, the festive choruses frenetic, the noise empty, the solo lamentations sentimental. How had I lost the clear movement from joy to fear to sadness? Where had the tension gone?

My first reaction was to want to quit composing. It's always demoralizing to watch a piece that seemed so promising fall apart. It feels like having the flu. But after much listening, talking to the performers, and letting some time pass, I realized what was wrong. I'd overindulged myself. The section was too full. There were too many dances, too many violent cymbals and drums, and too many sad laments. They canceled one another out. They stole the mystery from one another. I weeded out what I felt were the least effective songs in each category, cut the length of the happy dances, composed variations for the violent outbursts, and reduced the sad laments to one culminating prayer. Since I know myself, I can usually be sure that I'll overwrite, but despite years of experience, I rarely can catch the problem until I've created it.

Most of the arts in recent years have reflected a tendency toward understating or withholding emotion. But if you decide to write a musical piece about love, rage, or longing, it's important not to confuse your stylistic reticence with the internal life of your subject. If a piece of music comes across as cold or disjointed, chances are you haven't developed your rhythmic and melodic ideas fully enough. You've let the idea of minimalism get in between you and the actual music you've written. This is comparable to representing the song of the whale with its exact variables, toots, pauses, and hours of silence without trying to discover the *why* of its magic.

It's difficult to listen to one's own work objectively. With deadlines, stress, competition, it becomes doubly so. Therefore you should begin to cultivate friendships with a few strong souls who share your musical opinions, are generally supportive, but aren't afraid to speak their minds. Sometimes inviting an objective body into your rehearsal simply serves the purpose of putting your own judgment into a more critical mode. And as you get more confident and experienced, you will learn the limitations of even the finest critique. I have one friend, the producer Joseph Papp, of the Public Theater in New York, who is brilliant at pointing his finger on the structural or expressive weaknesses of a first draft. His way of giving critique, however, is disconcerting. He supplies the solutions, suggesting whole new characters, thematic possibilities, and other instruments. When he first started helping me with my work, I took him quite literally and tried to take into account his imaginative solutions. Now I realize that his variations on my themes were his way of expressing a feeling that one or another aspects of my work hadn't developed sufficiently or was redundant. His instincts were amazing, but his style of teaching was to try to rewrite my music and text for me.

Recently he and I were working on an opera I'm composing about Esther. After listening to my first version, he thought I should set the story in a Fifth Avenue apartment inhabited by Yuppies. If I'd followed his imaginative but completely zany ideas, I'd still be writing arias for Haman, the corrupt Wall Street banker. Instead I let his critique sink in, and analyzing it in my own terms, I realized he was frustrated by the lack of a clear context.

Telling the story of Esther without defining when, who, and why turned the characters into bad children's theater, weakened the themes of the story, and made the musical style arbitrary. When I wrote *The Haggadah*, an oratorio based on the Passover holiday and the Book of Exodus, I clearly set the work in the world of a village on the day before the first-night seder. Because of the timeless nature of the holiday in which Jews re-create symbolically the flight from Egypt, the liturgical references in the score were integral to it. The singers could move easily back and forth between biblical figures like Moses, Aaron, Pharaoh, and contemporary tellers of the story because we knew that they were preparing for Passover. The work ended with the "family" of performers seated around a seder table.

The Book of Esther has the carnival of Purim for me to draw from. I have recently finished a final draft, which has modern-day homeless beggars "crashing" a feast that a wealthy George Burns and Gracie Allen type couple are hosting for the audience. The beggars tell the story of

Esther in exchange for food and warmth. The carnival and feast aspect of the holiday supplies me with a reason for any kind of high-spirited dance music I want. The invasion of the poor performers into the house of the rich is a custom well known among Jews as the Purimspiel. Because my beggars live in 1988, they can pull their storytelling material and styles from any era of history they choose. Because Purim is a time for drinking, and hallucinating, the actors switch styles of song, characters, and sexes, and it is in keeping with the festival. Esther the queen is trying to save her poor abused people, and she is a feisty superhero. Mordechai is her superhero lover/fellow spy. The anti-Semite Haman shall be destroyed and the Jews and audience saved. Now and then actors interrupt each other and tell different versions of the story. The audience is required to participate and vote on preferred interpretations. The piece is entirely sung: the music tells the story. It is unpredictable, fast paced, and makes fun of itself.

I found this solution by keeping close to the Book of Esther and the many traditional songs and stories associated with the holiday. I decided to continually involve the audience as if I were creating a musical circus. This is a far cry from Joseph Papp's Upper East Side cocktail party, but he is the force who helped me move forward. Now the score of *Esther* can be Persian, Hebraic, contemporary rock, and reggae, and I don't have to justify my choices. Because Papp is a constructive critic, he won't begrudge me my own ideas and will applaud any solution that works.

A young composer must know whom to ask for comments. Listening to too many advisers is as bad as not asking anyone. One of my friends is highly informed and articulate about the avant-garde. Therefore she is invaluable when I work on operas like the La Mama trilogy or a ballet score. However, I've learned to not invite her to rehearsals of my rock shows because she's simply turned off by rigorous displays of direct emotion. Politics are not artistic to her, and although I'll argue with her privately, I don't want to waste time and feelings as she rips my less abstract works to shreds. Also, a young composer should examine the motivations of people who scan early drafts or come to run-throughs. The director Harold Clurman told his actors that they had no "friends" on an opening night. I think what he meant by this was simply that artists must accept that even the most well-intentioned friend or relative views a work from a backlog of experiences, associations, and wishes. Therefore, advice about rewriting ought to be carefully balanced against the personality and experience of the character who gives it. Don't expect a commercial record producer who's interested in *Billboard* charts and hummable hooks to be supportive of a ballet score written for cellos and chimes. However, if the person is respectful and skilled in his own field, there may be something gained in enduring his displeasure.

Ultimately a composer must sift and sort through comments and advice, her own and the auditor's, and go off alone to make the changes she will live with for the rest of the piece's life. Rewriting is an essential part of composing. An uneven first draft is rarely an unfortunate bit of bad luck that only accompanies a problematic piece. I don't think the structure of our performing institutions allows enough time for trial and error. Therefore a young composer should learn to schedule her working life to give breathing space for the evolution of her music. Too many composers, fraught with pressures for money and recognition, give in to schedules based solely on economic considerations. The result is that some of our best talent is producing careless and haphazard music. As a composer you should learn to revel in the solitary times with your work, when you reevaluate and reshape raw impulses into finished products. Though you are anxious to hear your work aloud, this is the time you can experience the delicious solitude of creation. Privacy and time bring new perspectives and ways to utilize your skills.

One of the hardest tasks the young composer has to learn is the art of cutting. When you've lived with an idea a long while, spent hours of time scratching out notes or overdubbing tracks, the attachment to the sounds becomes very deep. They are, after all, your creations. Many composers feel a sense of birth after finishing a piece, then a postpartum emptiness because that which lived inside you is now a separate living being out in the world. Sometimes composers will rewrite far past the point where it is necessary, just so they don't have to let go. (I have a friend who's been working on the same material for almost fifteen years.) But for the most part, composers have healthy exhibitionist streaks and want to show their "babies" off.

Still, the attachment can make cutting unbearable. The first act of *Runaways* was originally two hours long. The musical contained so many songs that were vital to my vision of childhood, my perception of street sounds, and the child's solitary struggle against the impossible home. Not all the songs were of equal vitality, and by the end of act 1, I'd lost the concentrated, urgent rhythm of the musical. Cutting songs was arduous and painful because I'd associated each one with a child in the company as well as an aspect of my own personality. Ultimately, I had to do what was good for the show, and the transition from nurturer to rejecter was agonizing. Later on in my career, when I was doing *Doonesbury,* I'd grown strong enough to be able to cut two very good songs because I realized they confused the forward motion of the show. I also knew that I'd use their melodies later on in some other context.

Theater, film, and TV composers learn to cut their material because they are subject to the imperatives of producers and conditions of contracts that give them no power. They must learn to work within this system without cynicism, finding a balance between fighting back and capitulating. Classical and jazz composers have to learn to engage in rigorous dialogue with their own egos. I imagine it is very difficult to be objective in these areas, especially when a composer is experimenting with forms that have little precedent.

The issue of cutting becomes important beyond whether a piece of music is too long or heavy. You have to be able to fall out of love with yourself in order to put the musical creation above your defensive opinions and sentiments. Finding this detachment, along with learning not to be compliant to the point of spoiling your work, is perhaps one of the aspects of composing that can never be emphasized enough, nor completely learned.

There are some basic signs that a cut is in order, and it's good to face them as early as possible before the attachment becomes too deep. Are you repeating an intensity too much? Are you repeating a theme with variations that don't illuminate or open the theme up? Are you going off in a direction that is exciting and new, but veers too far from the progression of your musical statement? Is it taking you too long to complete a statement? Do you have so many bright, interesting musical inventions going on that they distract from each other? Are there too many verses, choruses, bridges, endings? Does every instrument have to take a solo? Have you taken too long to set the mood before getting into the action of the music? Are you staying too long in an area of musical excitement, building the tension and conflict into chaotic noise? Have you finished what you wanted to say and begun a whole new thought simply because you didn't want to stop writing?

Pitfalls such as these are normal, and I don't know a composer whose work I admire who hasn't fallen into one of them. The key, I think, is to be on guard against the tendency to overwrite. The notion of wrong and right in music is subjective, but a keen ear, clear head, and honest evaluation are tools of the trade. No one should be so fragile that she can't pick up an eraser or hit the rewind/erase button. Now and then, accidents lead to whole discoveries. The twelfth song I wrote for *The Beautiful Lady* was completely out of place with the approach I'd taken in the show. The song was more modern in tone, harsher and darker in its melodic strains. Up until that time the score had been folk/oriented, rooted in Russian country music. I tried to cut the new song, and then realized what I really should cut were the other eleven. This event occured six months into the creation of the piece. I hated myself, but couldn't ignore what had to be done.

Many composers experience these turnarounds, and you must be courageous enough to follow the truth; even if the truth leads you to write twelve more songs in the new mode, then tells you to cut those songs and return to the original idea. The art of composing becomes more grounded, more like real work, when you're willing to take this approach. You learn to nurture yourself by the creative pleasures of your daily work rather than live in a fantasy world obsessed only with the final outcome.

SEVEN

Surviving Until...

THE ODDS AGAINST HAVING a satisfying and productive
career as a composer might make playing the lottery a more
sensible vocation for a young person. It is, in some ways, a
war that cannot be won, in which you are bound to be
wounded, and most likely to be paid a pittance for your
efforts. There has to be a fierce will to battle the odds, for
you can live an entire lifetime and never hear a single note
of your own music performed in public. But since you are
reading this book, you probably see yourself as a prospective
warrior, and in that case, you need to know how to survive
in this taxing profession. First, however, let me catalog some
of the negative aspects of a composing career so that you
know, quite specifically, what you are getting into.

Perhaps you are a classical composer. As you may know,
the repertoire of most symphony orechestras qualifies them
for museum status. Should they take on any new music, it is
generally at the rate of about one piece per season and is
booked two years in advance. Usually it comes to the
attention of the symphony's musical director through a
friend of a friend, and the choice is likely based not on any
true interest in new work but on the fact that a particular
kind of new music is "in" at the moment. An unsolicited or
unsponsored score seldom reaches a musical director, and
almost never is he so struck by its genius that he commits
himself to its performance.

144

There is occasionally a flash of light in this unrelieved bleakness. The conductor Serge Koussevitzky was a champion of new music. Pierre Boulez, himself a composer, opened up opportunties for new work during his time as director of the New York Philharmonic, especially of the atonal and electronic variety. Michael Tilson Thomas, Lukas Foss, and other major conductors present new music that gibes with their personal taste. But for the most part, new music falls on the deaf ears of the musical establishment.

Some orchestras do have so-called new music programs. Here again, political connections determine to a large degree who gets played, when, and how. These programs tend, at least outside of large cities, to be sparsely attended, and the listeners often don't like what they hear. Should the audience like the music (meaning they don't get up and leave at the earliest opportunity), it may be done again in five years, or ten.

The new music programs attached to universities are kinder to composers, but their performance schedules are limited, and the composer is usually paid little or nothing. These programs are most often dependent on foundation grants, for given the policies of the current administration, federal support has dwindled to a new low. So while your music might be played in a university setting with appreciation, and perhaps even understanding, you likely will still be carrying a sandwich for your lunch.

The museum mentality dominates the opera world even more than it does the concert world. New operas are rarely commissioned. If one is, you may be certain that it will not be produced for at least three years. There is a wonderful organization called Opera America that is attempting to make opera companies aware of composers other than Verdi, Puccini, Wagner, and Mozart, but it is an uphill fight, and as few as three new operas a year are performed under its auspices. The Houston and Minneapolis companies have begun programs to develop new operas, but they only have funding for developing a handful of operas, and of these only one or two will ever be performed nationally.

Jazz composers and players meet with a kind of neglect that has historically driven them to alcohol or drug addiction. In the past, they were not considered legitimate by the classical music world, nor was their music accepted as part of the mainstream of popular music. While the artistry of jazz is now recognized by some authorities and given scholarly treatment in books and in university courses, that is no substitute for the joy of playing one's music at a gig, or for the satisfaction of having it recorded. Jazz composers and players almost never receive proper financial compensation and almost always earn a living by arranging other people's material or by playing in dance bands or recording sessions. Even the new trends in dance and performance art, exemplified by Meredith Monk and Bobby McFerrin, to collaborate with jazz artists, leave most jazz performers unknown because they cannot or will not "cross over."

Economical conditions in the musical theater have made it virtually impossible to put on a Broadway show for less than two million dollars. Ticket prices of forty and fifty dollars, needed to offset such an outlay, trigger extraordinary expectations in an audience—and in critics, for that matter. The Broadway musical is also expected to entertain the suburban audience and to flatter its conventional expectations. When a musical fails at that task, when it steps outside the prescribed formula, it generally closes in one night. A producer who has lost his backers two million dollars in one night is less receptive, less generous, to the next original idea that comes along.

Other arenas for musical theater—Off Broadway, Off-Off-Broadway, regional theater—which should be encouraging experimentation, seem increasingly to serve as auditions for the next step up the economic ladder. Perhaps a young composer does the music for an Off-Off-Broadway show and it is well received and goes to Off Broadway. Then, because Off Broadway is in effect an audition for Broadway, a whole different set of factors comes into play. The pressures within the institutional theater are for a hit, with all that that implies, because only the royalties and subsidiary rights from a hit musical are sufficient to make a profit in the institutional theater. It is unsubsidized by the government or by foundations.

The odds are slightly better for the prospective singer/songwriter in the rock field, but slightly better is a long way from good. The faces you see on MTV or in the windows of the record stores are still a minuscule minority. To break through in this field, you must get a band together and rent a place to practice where you won't bother the neighbors. You must then develop a distinctive enough sound so that someone will take an interest in you and help you make a demo. Once the demo is made, it must be given to the A and R people at a record company. Most companies also now require you to give them a video. By the time you come up with the funding to get the video made, you're probably five thousand dollars in debt, an insupportable situation unless you were born into a rich family—in which case you should count your blessings, but also know that you are not guaranteed any return whatsoever on the funds you have laid out. And should you be a woman, simply take all the negatives I've enumerated, multiply them by ten, and you'll have some idea of the odds you face in any of the above categories.

These are some of the hard realities of life as a composer. And probably anyone other than a compulsive, obstinate idealist would be put off by such a gloomy picture. But, thank God, people who deal with music have a tenuous relationship with reality to begin with. Certain aspects of music can be explained logically: hitting something makes a sound, and that breaks into predictable overtones, which then commune with other overtones, and so on. But there is no logical explanation for what music does to the senses once it hits. And a composer is much more likely to believe in a dream than in demonstrable reality, a dream that can serve his or her own hunger, even while it speaks to the unconscious of other people.

Let me emphasize that this dream should not be an excuse for becoming dark and despairing, or for sinking into bitterness when your music does not get performed. Nor is it something so enormous or bizarre that its realization is utterly beyond your control. Discard the image of Don Quixote tilting at windmills. Discard the trappings of martyrdom. There *are* ways that you can make your music exactly as you dream it, and you can do it without losing fifty pounds and living in Grand Central Station. But it takes hard work and perseverance and guts.

The first prerequisite to surviving as a composer is to understand what is possible in the short, as opposed to the long, term. Two immediate questions present themselves, and the first is how to earn a living, a matter that has nothing to do with your chosen profession because music will offer you few opportunites that would pay even part of your rent. If you can't accept this, think again about your career choice.

There are many ways to support yourself, some of which I've already mentioned: working in a box office, as an usher, as gopher for someone in the musical world. Some composers in time make a living copying music, learning the art of making a score look beautiful. Cab driving allows you to hear the tonalities of different people's voices and to listen to tapes on the deck. Any kind of job, from paralegal work to janitorial, is fine as long as it pays for your overhead and leaves some leisure in which to work. Teaching is a wonderful job but hard to come by.

The second immediate question that arises is how to keep your sanity in this situation. The answer is simple: you compose. Try, if possible, to arrange your work schedule to leave free the time when you write best. Then do it regularly. And because you will want to hear your music, keep in touch with a network of people who can help you to do so. Composing is, necessarily, one of the more social art forms. And however shy, or even misanthropic, you may be, recognize that there is a lively as well as necessary exchange to be had with other people who are interested in sound.

At the outset of your musical life, begin keeping a notebook in which you list everyone who crosses your musical path. Keep track of the friend you had in the third grade who wanted to play the guitar and went on to do it professionally. Or the keyboard player in the high school band who later studied at Juilliard. Or the member of your class who ended up in Toronto singing in lounge bars. You don't know if she sings well or not, but keep her name. Also keep the names of everyone who played cello, viola, violin, or trombone in college, or the members of all your college rock bands. These names are gold to you. You don't know what people have gone on to do, or what you may have in common with them. You may want to write a piece with Tibetan gongs, and you discover that Dougie Howard, who sat next to you in band in the horn section, has become a percussionist. When I was becoming acquainted with synthesizers, I learned that one of my dearest friends from college had become an expert in computer programming at Stanford University. He'd had no connection with computers when I knew him. Take an interest in the human race and in what is going on around you. When you do, you may eventually end up with a private group or even orchestra at your disposal.

Must you pay these people each time they perform for you? No. Musicians who are just starting out have not yet joined a union local and won't demand pay for every job. They are exploring, just as you are. And this is sometimes true of experienced players as well. I've known remarkable, seasoned players to put away their vocational attitudes and stay beyond a recording session to play something new because they were interested in the music. A leading jazz musician, a woman who can name her own gigs and has her own band, did *Jerusalem* because she had never played that kind of music before and she loved the people she was working with. You never know.

Taking ticket orders at Ticketron, copying an older composer's music, running a broom around a floor and wanting to weep, or leading aerobic exercises to a beat you abhor will be more bearable if you know that between nine and eleven o'clock that night you are going to live in a world of your own performed sound. And however often this happens, if it's three times a week or only once a month, it's very important that you approach it in a disciplined way. Don't spend time thinking about how happy you are to be hanging out with musicians. Have an agenda, know what you want to rehearse, what you want to hear, how to get it, how to criticize. This is not a democratic situation: you are the leader and should behave that way. Get the job done, do it cheerfully, and then celebrate.

And accept that this is your milieu for the present. Have the highest regard for your long-range capabilites, but work with the realities of the here and now. Write a full symphony, if you like, but don't write only that if you only have half a dozen musicians available. Stretch your musical boundaries as far as you wish—a classical composer needn't be limited to writing quartets, nor a songwriter to writing five demo tunes, nor a jazz ensemble to the sounds of one set—but make sure you write something that will sustain you in the present. If you write only the one large symphony, and you then undergo the tedious, often futile process of attempting to get it into appropriate hands, you will most likely end up with only disappointment to show for your efforts. And should you, by accident, be the one in ten thousand who makes it the first time out, this doesn't guarantee further success, though temporarily it feels like it does. To survive in the musical world, as I said, you need guts. And you need spiritual strength. A quick success can rob you of the opportunity to develop inner fortitude and the penchant to experiment and grow. And when you need them later on, they won't be there.

All composers would like to lie back and dream their music and, magically, have it produced by someone else. Producing, and all it entails, does not suit the composing temperament. Unfortunately, conditions are such that if you want your music to be heard, you will most likely have to produce it yourself. The age of the musical patron is over, and even should it dawn again, only a small number of artists would be subsidized in any case. Having your music heard verifies that all the time, thought, and spirit you spent were worth it if people do respond to your music with some warmth. It also verifies that you are not mad, that the sounds you hear in your head are indeed sounds that move others, too.

The minimal skills you need in order to produce are the ability to write a letter, to make a phone call, to make connections. Be shameless about this last item. Does anyone—family, friends, near strangers—know anyone who could be helpful? Pursue them. Steal any little cardboard invitation that you come across and go to receptions and parties and talk to people. Attend art gallery openings and ask anyone who strikes your fancy to come and hear your music. Remember that the first priority is to get heard by as many people as possible. When your finer instincts tell you that your behavior is cold and calculating, dishonest, hateful, parasitic—all those adjectives the so-called pure artists like to attach to such activities—ignore them. Pursuing people and putting your music forward does not mean that you're Sammy Glick; it does not mean that you can't be polite; it does not mean that you're hypocritical. It simply means that part of your task is to get people to listen to your music, and to do that you need to seek them out and interest them.

You need also to find a place where these people can come to listen. Galleries sometimes have music performances. Some community centers sponsor musical programs. There are loft spaces all over the country where music can be performed. Cafeterias and gymnasiums in schools might be available. Storefronts in downtown areas are other places to explore. Renting a performance space requires saving up some money. So lay off drugs. Don't buy the new sweater you've been coveting. Hock some of your old schoolbooks. Be inventive. Have a friend who is a graphics major help you put together a flier. One way or another, get the music heard. And after it's been heard twenty or thirty times, perhaps someone will come to your aid and support. If not, it doesn't mean that you don't do good work. It does mean, however, that you must evaluate whether or not you're willing to keep working this way, because being discovered on any level can take a very long time.

Every young composer must own a decent tape recorder and be able to put together a simple, clear cassette not more than half an hour long that gives a good representation of his or her style. I'll discuss later the specific requirements for different kinds of music, but adhere to the general rule that once you're in contact with really good musicians, you should make a tape. And here again, be inventive. Street musicians are back in vogue, for instance, so finagle some of your musician friends into including a piece of yours in their sidewalk concert, move in close with your recorder, and get it on tape.

Go to the library and look up in a foundation guide all the organizations that give music grants. Explore the grants that are offered by either the state or federal government. Fill out applications and submit them with your tape. Duplicating tapes can be expensive, but perhaps you can do something for a studio and they will copy your tapes in return. I have friends who have invested in studio-quality recorders, and they record and put the tapes together themselves. It may end up being cheaper to have the studio in your own home. Don't give in to difficulties as they arise. Don't let your little chest sink. If you send out one hundred applications, you might get a grant. It's not likely to come your way the first time around, but it could happen and it's silly to overlook the chance. Also, it lays the groundwork for your later musical life, when you will continue to apply as a less anonymous candidate. The more times you apply, the more noticeable you become.

If you're sending a tape to a record, film, or television company, an agency, or an organization that develops musical theater projects, include a cover letter that contains recommendations from other people who work in the field. This is a place where you will use those connections you have been cultivating.

Once you have done this, remember that it doesn't do any good to nag. Tactics used in those scenes from movie musicals in which the eager young artist camps on the doorstep and makes fifteen phone calls a day will not be productive in real life. A follow-up letter asking if the tape was received and another letter three months later asking if the tape has been heard are appropriate. A few months after that, you should write to say that if they have not liked the tape, would they please send it back. Be courteous in these communications; it never hurts to remind people to use good manners. At the same time, don't let them ignore you. It's not good for you, for them, or for the next person who comes along. It is their job to listen, and they should not be too busy to do their job.

If you wangle an actual appointment with any of these people, be able to say concisely what your music is about, bring a tape with you, or, if you perform it live, do it cleanly and simply. Do not try to schmaltz it up; remember you are selling your music and your ideas, not yourself.

Other outlets to explore are BMI (Broadcast Music Incorporated) and ASCAP (American Society of Composers, Authors, and Publishers). They have a variety of programs that showcase young composers and bring them together with other composers and with performers. There are also songwriters' associations in all parts of the country advertised in *Rolling Stone, Down Beat,* or other music magazines. Opera America, which I mentioned earlier, publishes a newsletter that keeps abreast of new and experimental endeavors in the operatic and musical theater worlds. It also serves as a match maker, bringing opera company directors into contact with composers. Sometimes residences with a company and commissions result from these meetings. Opera America also keeps opera companies apprised of the grants available to underwrite new works. Programs for musical theater exist at the Mark Taper Forum in Los Angeles, the Louisville Theater Company, the O'Neill Playwrights Conference in Connecticut, the Sundance Institute in Utah, and in Lenox, Massachusetts, in the summer, and many other places. Joseph Papp always encourages new musicals at the Public Theater and he especially invites rock and roll and other contemporary composers to contribute their work. Ellen Stewart of La Mama is first among international theater composers, with companies in New York, Paris, Italy, North Africa, Buenos Aires, and Manila, and with musicians spread out all over Africa and the Far East. There are jazz composition contests, jam sessions, songwriting workshops, experimental music ensembles, internships, and independent record labels advertised in music magazines, on club bulletin boards, and in college newspapers. Make it your business to know about these programs that encourage experimentation and support new work.

As your own producer, you must learn how to make a budget. This is not as daunting as it may seem, and if you can't estimate the expenses, find a friend who can. Know the cost of rental space for rehearsal (if this item is too steep for you, be wily once more and do a favor for someone who has an appropriate space), how many musicians you'll need and their fees, if any, the amount and cost of the tape you'll need. If you're going to be transcribing, how much will manuscript paper cost? If someone else is going to transcribe, figure the cost of that labor. How much money will you need to spend on stamps and mailing envelopes to send things out?

Punk rock groups have made a valuable contribution to all musicians by producing their own records and showing that it can be done cheaply and well. When I was growing up in Buffalo, places existed that would press a 78 or an unwieldy 33⅓ for about twenty-five dollars. Obviously, it would be much more expensive today, and you would want a better quality than this operation offered, but ways do exist to get this done relatively inexpensively. Explore them. Many young composers save up for their own Teac four-track Portastudio and synthesizer sequencer, which is capable of playing back multilayered compositions.

If you are working in the classical field, you will submit a manuscipt rather than a tape. Conductors pride themselves on being able to hear what they see on a page. But, as I noted in the third chapter, elegance and clarity of notation are crucial. Your score, which communicates your musical intention, must look beautiful on the page. You will most likely submit your manuscript to a musical director or to an agency or artists' management concern, like William Morris or ICM or Columbia Artists, which will try to bring your composition to the attention of a conductor. Decide for yourself what works best in your approach to these organizations. Perhaps an unvarnished presentation of yourself will be effective. Perhaps you'd do better to put on a bit of show: a black overcoat with a white silk scarf, hair in a chic style, a pallid expression or a sultry one, a nice executive business suit or clean blue jeans, a cable-knit sweater, or a red leather miniskirt and lace camisole, depending on the environment—jolly in the face of adversity or fiercely courageous with only a slight tremble of lip to indicate underlying angst. Don't be afraid to ham it up a bit, and if you choose to, don't judge yourself harshly for it. Composers are, after all, performers.

Classical and jazz composers should also be aware of music festivals, competitions, and what is going on musically at universities. Find out who is in charge of the different programs and, if need be, present your manuscript yourself. The worst that can happen is that someone will say no, you are talentless, this is not music. Get used to such brutal outspokenness. Music is a visceral art form, and musical people tend to respond to it fervidly. You will rarely encounter someone who says, for instance, "Sorry, but it's just not for me."

Not only must you be your own producer, you must be your own agent as well. There are exceptions to this: classical composers who are represented by one of the three agencies I mentioned, clients of the Hollywood agencies that handle the big names in film scoring, a certain kind of musical theater composer. But agents really don't quite know what to do with composers who fall outside this select company. The main reason for this is economic. A young composer might beam with pride at his or her output, which includes a score for a low-budget independent film, five PBS programs, an Off-Broadway musical, and a ballet, but an agent looking at the same properties will know that a 10 percent take of this style of artist might come to a few hundred dollars a year for all the years that may go by before her first feature or miniseries. Many agents are low on patience.

Kander and Ebb, Marvin Hamlisch, and John Williams are good examples of the kind of composers that agents are eager to represent. They make lots of residuals and have gained a certain celebrity status. But this doesn't mean they were born into recognition and that ICM or William Morris sought them out before their successes. Philip Glass is now in that category, but his current fortune did not come fast or easily. Ten years ago, you wouldn't find agents saying "like a Philip Glass." We are living in the era of the personality cult. Some composers survive by taking solace in a sequestered university environment, but most of us have had to learn to sell our product. Ambition requires that the purist in you will compromise, not your aesthetics but your attraction to the solitary musical life.

So learn how to represent yourself and master the pitching techniques I've mentioned. Educate yourself with regard to the practical details of getting music played, and expect that you will be turned down again and again. That is the reality, so find a way to accept it. And disabuse yourself of the notion that being rejected is the most painful thing that can happen to you. Much more painful is having a piece performed badly and, as a consequence, destroyed.

Yes, in the minefield of a composing career, there are dangers to acceptance, too. Let's say you finish a piece of music with a trembling hand and send it off to a well-known conductor. You pray for the day when he says yes, and that day, astonishingly enough, arrives. The conductor then chooses the musicians who will play your piece and the place where it will be performed, and he rehearses and performs the music according to his own interpretation. Basically, what you get to do is come and listen to it. The first time this happens, you will most likely be in a fog of ecstatic disbelief. Is this really happening? The first time I heard someone sing a piece of my music, I thought I would pass out. But generally, after this initial blush of exhilaration, a period of caution that lasts several decades sets in because nothing, at least at first, sounds right.

I feel strongly that there is no excuse for older performers and conductors abusing younger composers, and that it is the composer's job to make sure it doesn't happen. Part of being a composer is being responsible for the proper performances of your music. You must know how to get the sounds you want. If you are fortunate enough to conduct your own music, there is a good chance of this happening. But it won't happen by magic. You must be prepared to use every technique, short of physical abuse, to pull from the conductor and musicians what you need. Cajole, scream, flatter, use verbal descriptions, or demonstrate yourself—do whatever it takes. If you are not prepared to do so, you have no right to expect anything. Getting angry and sulking when you've made no effort to get what you want either from a conductor, musical director, or group of musicians is cowardly.

If you are a shrinking violet, unable to leave your house, you must still take responsibility for your music sounding the way you want it to. Hook up with a musical director you trust and with whom you can argue. Let the musical director, who is more aggressive than you are and who deals well with conductors and musicians, serve as your stand-in.

The best way to ensure that your music is played right is to pick your musicians and work with them yourself. I've done this from the beginning of my career, and while some might dismiss it as an impossibility, I'm convinced that young composers are more likely to be heard, and heard accurately, this way than by pursuing other kinds of performance opportunities.

I have always wanted to know who my musicians were, what kind of personalities they had. Would they practice five hours a day? Did they have a sense of humor? Was their pitch good, and their tone? Could they make a cello sound like a tamboura? If they didn't know what a tamboura was, would they listen to one? These considerations have always seemed more important to me than someone's experience or fame. Rather than seeking out "names," I've looked for people who were workers and who would respond to me and my music. Where would I find people like that? Where was it realistic to think I could get my music done? If a group of six-year-olds humming my music on kazoos in a grammar school would listen to me and hear what I had to say, I would rather work with them than with a diva at the Met, if working with her meant adjusting my vision to her idiosyncrasies. At least, in the former situation, I would be in control, and if I was in control, my sound would come out exactly as I wished, and then people would come to me.

This may sound self-destructive, but in some ways it is just the opposite. Central to my way of thinking is the conviction that any musical composition, unlike a novel or a poem, is ultimately a collaboration. A piece of music is nothing without the person who performs it. No piece of music stands on its own. If Janet Baker sings a song her way, and Joan Baez sings the same song her way, the music will be different. It will become what the performer does to it. If music were a reading art, we could dispense with musicians and everyone could go to libraries and read scores. But it isn't; it must be heard.

Since composition is not a solo effort, it is crucial for a composer to know who is doing his or her music. If you are working in the musical theater, take part in the casting. Have your contract stipulate that you are to be included in this process. Even if it's your first show, don't let gratitude make you passive or irresolute. Insist on your input, and again, use your own musicians whenever you can. If someone suggests a percussionist from the Philharmonic to play a jazz solo, put your foot down quietly but firmly. Simply say: "This is who I had in mind to do this piece." Don't crawl about after this superstar or that diva. American musical performance in particular is deteriorating because of the worship of the big name, and many young, ambitious composers are seduced by the trappings of glittery stars and institutions rather than demanding the input of a musical collaboration. If you focus on big names and splashy concertizing, I can assure you that your love for music will fade rapidly. However, if you are a real composer who looks forward to a long, creative life, you will concentrate on the music itself, finding people to play it the way you hear it, giving them full credit for their artistry, growing with them, and cherishing them and the moments when the music gets made.

As I have said, it is difficult to earn a living writing music, and sooner or later every composer faces the issue of compromise. What kind of composing are you willing to take on for economic reasons? There are essentially three attitudes toward this question. The first is the purist stance, which allows no compromise whatsoever. I think of it as the ascetic version of survival, and I mistrust it most of all. People who think the voice of God has summoned them to a higher calling than the rest of mankind make me uneasy in any situation.

The second attitude is at the other extreme, and it is held by people who have taken on a lot of commercial jobs at which they're quite good and have conned themselves into believing that they can drop these at any time and return to their "real" work. It won't happen. The life-style the commercial world makes available is as addictive as cocaine. Also, you will get used to appealing to the lowest common denominator of taste, and so competing, say, to write the theme song for the sequel to "Miami Vice" will become an opportunity of paramount importance.

The third attitude, the one held, I hope by readers of this book, allows some room for economic realities but not at the expense of your inner vision, those sounds that awakened you when you were five and let you know you weren't like everyone else because you heard musical subtleties in the events of life. Your primary commitment is to these sounds, but you also recognize that you must stay physically and mentally healthy, and if a chance comes along to relieve some financial stress by doing an ad jingle, there is nothing wrong with taking it and doing a good job. Approach it as a student. Find out exactly what goes on in this world, and see what you can learn from it. Find out about synthesizers, recording values, and how recording studios operate, and pay attention to the hotshot sight readers you'll encounter because some of the greatest singers do jingles. Perhaps one day you'll write something one of them will like, and he or she will perform for you.

Or maybe you compromise and agree to do some work on a student film that pays you a few hundred dollars and covers your rent for the month. Again, see what you can learn from this, and recognize that the young director you're working with may grow into someone with an interesting sensibility and, eventually, the wherewithal to make feature films. That has happened to me. I've stuck with the people I began with, watched them grow, and moved from half-hour films with a little incidental music here and there to full-length television movies and feature films. On the way, I learned how to use a stopwatch and a click track, to score to the picture onscreen, to underline the subtext in a scene by orchestration, to help a weak character musically, to soften one who's too tough. These skills can lead you into an

area of legitimate composition that can also be quite lucrative. Though it's very difficult to break in to the all-male
elite that is responsible for the scores of most major Hollywood films, there are many fine independent films being
made today by men and women who want the music that
accompanies their films to be of the highest quality.

When you consider a job for economical reasons, ask
what the cost will be to you in time and energy, and weigh
whether or not it is worth it. For instance, to get film score
work, about which I'll say more later, the customary proce-
dure is to put together a tape that shows your stylistic range:
a chase scene, a love scene, a discovery scene, perhaps a
Welsh childhood scene because you've heard about an
upcoming miniseries based on the life of Richard Burton. If
you're facile enough so that putting this together will take
just a few days, do it. A single film job can support a
substantial period of writing your own music. If it's difficult
for you to write in many different styles, however, and
making such a tape would take you ten weeks, don't do it.

Let's say the possibility arises of doing incidental music
for a documentary, or someone offers you a job doing a
video, or a friend from college has become a choreographer
and gotten a grant and has three hundred dollars to spend on
a fifteen-minute ballet score. Ask yourself if the enterprise
will help you grow in any way. Will you learn anything from
it? Is the subject one you might write about anyway? Is it one
you think you can handle? Do you simply need the money?
Any of these is a valid reason for taking a job, but be clear
about your motives. And don't fall into the trap of thinking
that commissioned work is somehow more valuable than
self-motivated composition.

I've had periods in my life in which I was convinced
that the music other people wanted me to write was more
legitimate than the music I wrote at home, for myself, that
nobody wanted, at least not then. It's easy to get your values

mixed up when you're offered scores by two filmmakers, ballets by a couple of choreographers, and incidental music for an avant-garde theater company, and a friend wants you to write a song for his wedding, and all of them pay you for your efforts. Acceptance in the social circles of the music world can be seductive, especially in contrast to the isolated, lonely way you labor at the work that has been with you since you became a composer. Be cautious of this when you compromise for the sake of financial security. And remember your primary commitment. Your own music is a mystery and an adventure. It's always possible that it could be an enormous failure. But it could also be a miracle. If you lose the recognition of that, and the center it gives you, you lose the reason you began to write music in the first place.

When you seek to answer the question of compromise for yourself, give some weight to the romantic notion of sacrificing all for your art. There are times, I think, when it is appropriate to give up everything for a lover, a fight for justice, or a piece of music. The kind of passion that sparks this motive is a necessary part of human experience. At the same time, it is not necessary to build an entire life around sacrifice. I take no comfort from knowing that Bartok died, unknown, in a hotel, or that Charlie Parker was ignored when he wasn't on top anymore, or that Jim Morrison and Janis Joplin self-destructed at an early age. The list of composers and musicians who have succumbed either to their own or to society's destructive impulses is a disturbing reflection of the public's romance with the demoniac music maker. I'd prefer to fight to change these repeated scenes, rather than play them myself. I don't find suicide glamorous or malnutrition necessary. Learn to strike some kind of balance between the practical realities of life and the spiritual demands of your music. There is a big difference between the occasional compromise and music-is-a-business as a way of life.

Perhaps you want to be a composer who writes mainly jingles, or the music that goes inside a singing dolly or a computer game, or the tunes for a set of Cabbage Patch sing-along records. Or perhaps you write Musak music, which causes people to work faster, soothes them in an elevator, or prods them to buy more at a department store counter. Or maybe you write industrial music, something for American Airlines, for instance, about the twenty-five countries they fly to. None of these is easy to do. All of them require certain gifts. But they constitute commercial art, consumer art, and any composer who does this kind of work should be clear that he or she is engaged in making a living, not composing.

It is also business, not art, when a Michel Legrand imitator, for example, writes a movie score with Michel Legrand signature strings, and is doing so because he was told "the music should be like . . ." Whether the pretender is producing the strings on a synthesizer or using the same telling chord progressions on sustained piano notes, the subliminal trick is always there; lushly sentimental, filled with nostalgia, telegraphing messages about who will die, who will live, which romance will bite the dust, which will flourish. Imitators who specialize in copying what is already manipulative music become facile at this and will manufacture movie themes in a very businesslike, "do it exactly like . . ." way. Some composers believe they are writing from the heart, but their passion for formulas and sounding *like* a money-making composer gets confused with real musical inspiration. Soap opera music is a business, and the people who supply it know exactly what they're doing, what kind of flourish accompanies the announcement "I'm pregnant," what kind goes with "I'm pregnant but I have no intention of having the baby," what kind suits a really portentous announcement: "I was pregnant, I had an abortion, and the doctor who performed it was the father."

Something that is created for reasons of commerce can never be the same as something that is created to explore the spirit. And the more completely and deeply an art form is used to explore, scold, celebrate, and polemicize about the human race, the more important the work is. A formulated, packaged album of sentimental mail-order hits is not as important to the nurturing and growth of mankind as music that awakens the spirit and causes people to contemplate the horrors of a fascistic government, the terrible things men and women can do to each other in the name of love, the wrongs that children suffer, the astonishment of a child's first years on earth, the wonder of loving someone, or the humorous and poignant fantasies of welfare hotel kids.

The market research that makes money and passes for entertainment on Broadway is not superior to the small show that begins in a basement, put together by people convinced there are great possibilities in the story of a shoemaker in Vilna in 1810, the life of Emma Lazarus, the Joseph saga, stories of the Chilean counterrevolution, or the effort to capture in detail a family in an American Asian ghetto. But established composers who might tackle these kinds of subjects, take greater risks, try more subtle forms, attempt to break through the cliché-ridden, media-saturated sensibilities of the public, are stopped in their tracks by economics. And they repeat, and repeat, what has made them money in the past. Art and business do not mix, and when business is the motivating force, even unconsciously, when the artist cannot separate himself from the opportunity to make money, art dies. People say that Bach wrote his music for money, that it was his job. I don't believe it. I believe he did it for God.

Aside from general principles, there are particular things one needs to know to survive in certain fields. I mentioned earlier that film scoring is a legitimate area of composition, and one has only to listen to the scores of John Williams, Nino Rota, Bernard Herrmann, or Carmine Coppola to know this. In *Jaws*, it was the eerie heartbeat Williams created, rather than film images of the shark, that signaled its approach and built suspense. What an inspired musical choice. And in *Star Wars*, he wrote a score filled with patriotic feeling for a country that doesn't exist. That's not easy to do. Herrmann's brilliant music for *Psycho* was responsible for much of the terror in the shower scene. You really didn't see the killer do anything. This is especially evident if you listen to the music without seeing the images. Carmine Coppola's score for *The Black Stallion* was extraordinary. He was capable of creating deep family feeling and cold violence, wonder, mystery, and the galloping freedom of a mythical animal. Nino Rota, Fellini's longtime collaborator, reinvented the melancholy of circus music for *La Strada*, and he guided the whole brooding, nostalgic tone of *The Godfather*.

In order to write scores for film or television, you must accept the process of getting work, though it may go against your grain, as it does against mine. This means putting together an effective "reel" written in different styles. I don't like the idea of cutting into the middle of one piece and linking it with something utterly unrelated. I'm willing to talk at length to someone with a five-thousand-dollar budget for a film, the score for which would probably net me about two hundred. But I hate simply sending an anonymous tape of a lot of chopped up music to a billion-dollar movie studio. Nevertheless, I do it when I have to, concentrating on my editing as if it were composing, and I'm delighted as anyone when I get hired for a big job.

Film or television work can be lucrative, as I said, and it can also be highly educational, sometimes fun, occasionally marvelous if you're working on a good film with talented people. It teaches you how to create something worthwhile in thirty seconds, how to divide instruments so that they don't intrude on the drama, how to exercise such a delicate touch that no one knows your music is present, even as it produces an effect. You learn to deal with the values dictated by movie conventions: the music must swell in a love scene when two people kiss; how do you do this without sounding banal and overly sentimental? You learn how to work in a studio, how to mix, how mixing differs when there is just music or music combined with other sound tracks. You learn a great deal about orchestrating: how to orchestrate murders, love scenes, hate scenes, arguments, mischief, animation, funerals, weddings, chases, captures. You learn how to make something sound right in a very short time, how to do in a minute something you would have thought needed an hour.

When a scoring job is good, it can be very, very good, and when it's bad, it's horrid. Often on a feature film, there are half a dozen opinions that must be taken into account at every turn, half a dozen executives who have their musical preferences, and also have teenagers with distinct musical tastes whom they quote at meetings. Probably a few of them intended at one time to write music, and perhaps one of them does. Producers and directors of features may tell you that they're tone deaf and they're going to leave the music up to you, but this will not happen. They also think they know exactly what they want. Of course, even when they got what they think they want, they argue over it endlessly. You must have your ego firmly under control to survive in this kind of situation.

If you're working on a television movie, you will tend to run into strong biases and a general inclination toward hummable themes, minimum musical intrusion, and imitation. Someone will ride herd on you to make sure that you don't do anything too original, anything that sticks out, or anything too artsy. I once had a job writing the score for a television movie about Gauguin. We were down to the stage of the final mix, and the executive producer came in to hear the music. Having done some research, I used drums and voices that I deemed Tahitian in tone for Gauguin arriving in Tahiti. After listening briefly, the producer leaped up and exclaimed, "What is she doing making weird tribal music? I want strings. Strings!" (I learned, not surprisingly, that the producer's first choice had been Michel Legrand: beware of being second, third, or fourth choice because the powers that be rarely get over their first love.) A bit later, listening to the long cue that accompanied Gauguin's painting (a large mural, painted just before his death), the producer rose once more and hollered, "Now's she's sounding like Stravinsky. We don't want Stravinsky. We want strings. Strings!" My lawyer was called by the producer the next day, who said that I would be paid the minimum, and all of my music was being replaced. The music that finally accompanied the film was precisely the kind that lets you know instantly you are in the presence of a television movie.

If you're working in television, you will also be asked to make changes according to the following sort of directives: "Make it sound like 'Police Woman,' but not too much. Maybe there should be a little bit of 'Bullwinkle.' Yeah, do 'Police Woman' and 'Bullwinkle,' but not too much 'Bullwinkle.' Also, people now are really into that guy who plays sort of mystical music, so put in some of that stuff, and be sure you use a synthesizer. It's cheaper."

Worst of all is to be asked to do "carpeting," wall-to-wall music that exists from the beginning to the end of a program. In the heyday of Hollywood filmmaking, carpeting was common, and it was very effective; lush, heavily orchestrated, sweeping scores by composers like Max Steiner that provided about three-quarters of the expressive sound that took place in the film. There is a wonderful story told about Bette Davis, who was to do a scene in *Dark Victory* in which she ascended a grand staircase. Just after beginning, she stopped the action and said, "Excuse me, but before I do this I want to know if I'm going up the stairs or if Max Steiner is going up the stairs?" Today, however, carpeting generally consists of pulpy music of the sort that accompanies bad miniseries. It's a lot of work and seldom satisfying to write.

Another problematic condition for the composer in television is the high level of anxiety. The producers and directors act as though their jobs are in constant jeopardy. As soon as they hire you, they're terrified that you will do something that will ruin the entire project, even if your contribution consists of only three cues of twenty seconds apiece. Because of their anxiety, they check on you constantly.

The producers and directors of PBS projects are generally less intimidated and also more sensitive to the composer, concerned about the quality of the music, and eager to have it make a dramatic contribution. The atmosphere of these projects can often be genuinely creative, and I recommend it highly for young composers.

Also, there is an emerging group of young network executives who behave as disrespectfully as older executives, but who have a profound sense of music's power and therefore ask for more inventive composition. I recently completed an NBC miniseries called "A Year in the Life," and though the producer/writers were anxious about my participation, it was me they wanted. I had to rewrite themes many times over, listen to tapes of other scores, and absorb lectures on characters, instruments, schedules, and recording techniques; when in the studio, often I'd receive orders for last-minute changes and specific instruments in my earphones right before takes. Once or twice the associate producer hummed a suggestion for a theme or harmony over the studio call box, and once one of the producers wanted to conduct. These men were adamant about getting what they wanted, even if they discovered what that was only after they had heard it.

By the time I left Hollywood, I was exhausted, but I'd written a genuinely original score. I have to wonder at what cost. I turned down the offer to compose the full series because of a scheduling conflict. I have no idea how I would have survived a two-year stint under that kind of pressure, and I don't know if the search for original music would have continued week to week. But I don't want to stereotype the Hollywood scene. Many TV and movie producers love music and have a keen ear for what will serve their work. A composer has to know the difference between a passionate filmmaker and a power-hungry business executive.

Surviving in the pop or rock fields also calls for specialized savvy. To put together a demo that represents your sound, that identifying style filled with your energy and personality, can be done, as I've said, without a huge outlay of cash. Look for out-of-the-way studios, not well-known places that will charge you a year's salary for one tape. Learn at the beginning of your career to search out the bargains. By doing that, you'll also become expert at working with minimal means and equipment, and when the time comes that you're able to expand, you will still be able to maintain economy and simplicity in your music. The key to all good music is simplicity of intention and execution.

Synthesizers, tape decks, sequencers, and drum machines make it possible for a group of young people to share the ownership of a small studio. By engineering and playing for each other, you can put together a professional-sounding demo. If your sound is more raw and acoustic, a two-track or high-quality Sony can suffice. Laying down clear rhythm tracks and a balanced vocal, capturing a performance that reflects the energy of your musical act, is the first step toward approaching the world of records and clubs. In the areas of jazz, rock, and pop, we must talk about the composer as a composer/performer because this is more often than not the case. A composer/performer must find the band that works, not just in the studio, but live as well. He or she must be involved in finding bookings. Where are the clubs, restaurants, and after-hours bars that hire performers like you? Do you have to pepper your set with standards before introducing your own? Bob Dylan alternated between Woody Guthrie tunes and his own. Miles Davis played Charlie Parker. James Taylor played Carole King's songs. Judy Collins introduced Joni Mitchell, Dick Peaslee, Stephen Sondheim, and many others into the pop world before featuring her own songs. Other groups like Police or the Stones or Huey Newton have been lucky enough to be discovered for their performance style and original music. But you must evaluate your strengths and decide on a performance tactic. Some writers like Ellie Greenwich or Jimmy Webb stay behind the scenes. Whatever the choice, pop and rock music is a series of "scenes," and each scene requires a special kind of entry. Most pop and rock composer/performers end up with managers, who know clubs, disc jockeys, executives at record labels, concert booking agencies, and record producers.

A word to the innocent on that subject. The stereotype of the slippery, greedy rock manager, who wears dark glasses, is never alone, and operates with a kind of showy hustle, has some truth to it. A manager may seem competent in a business sense, and give you enough of an allowance to make you feel well taken care of, but the danger is that you might end up exploited. Often in the composer/performer–manager relationship, the performer becomes a dependent child and the manager takes profits or charges fees beyond what is ethical. Few music managers have the sensitivity to treasure a client's individuality. Many have been in "the business" a long time and think they know exactly how to shape a career. They will talk to a young composer about everything from repertoire to clothing. I once met a manager who listened to all my music, read my librettos, and told me I'd do better if I cut my hair and capped my front teeth. A friend of mine signed up with a man who charged him a monthly rate plus 10 percent of all earnings and, in a paternal manner, offered to option a series of my friend's songs for a movie score, which he said could sell as a concept album. The manager offered to pay one dollar for the songs because it would be a "deal of trust."

There's good reason why so many horror stories and lawsuits happen in the rock and pop arena. Since rock and pop (including country) composers are also performers, they start quite young, and are naive, whether in business or personal arrangements. Managers see hundreds of young people and hear twice as many demos. They're well aware of the hunger in the music world, and even the kindest of them have developed a cynicism toward the innocent composer/performers who want to break in. Their cynicism toward clients is equaled only by their suspicion of anyone else in the business. I've never met an agent or manager in the music business who doesn't give speeches about the danger and corruption of commercial music and everyone involved in it, except, of course, himself.

The exceptions in this field are godsends. I have a lawyer who's been with me since I was twenty-four. He's seen me through six agents and four managers. He is the rare kind of entertainment lawyer who's secure enough in his field to enjoy the adventure of representing new talents whether they yield a profit or not. He reads, goes to galleries, concerts, and the theater, and can recite whole passages from *Alice in Wonderland* and most of Shakespeare's sonnets. He is not as fond of my more violent works as he is of my more subtle and lyric ones, but he stands behind everything I do. He is a shark when it comes to protecting my deals, but understands if I give up a lucrative job for a more challenging commission. He collects his percentage when I have it and defers it when I don't. He yells at me when I'm arrogant, and comforts me when I'm humiliated. He's fallen asleep in a few of my shows and has never played the role of flatterer. I could have survived these years without him, but I think the quality of my work has deepened because I haven't had to suffer the total upheaval of losing representation, guidance, and a strong voice in my business choices. He plays as important a role in my creative history as any of my mentors. I've learned not to expect him to "sell" me, send around my résumé for jobs, or help me make the connections that will further my career.

A good relationship with a manager or agent requires that you don't make a parent of the man or woman who primarily guides your business interests. Hostile dependency is insulting to each party, and the relationship between manager and client can fall easily into this trap. There are good agents and managers to be found, men and women who care for artists and don't want them swallowed up by an inhumane system. The owners of the Bottom Line in New York, Allan Pepper and Stanley Snadowsky, are two such men. They are not agents but producers and entrepreneurs who have always supported young composers, performers, and writers. They are brave enough to try out new music, talent, and forms, and once they like someone, they stay loyal and interested. All over the country there are club owners, recording studio engineers, loft/gallery owners, small record producers, publishers, booking agents, and independent producers who take joy in good music. If you find you have a sweet-talking, hypocritical crook, chances are it was your ambition and naïveté that led you to him. Be careful not to sign long-term contracts with anyone, and watch out for phrases that commit you to paying percentages past your term of representation. The search for a reliable agent or manager is as rocky as finding a good marriage. It might take several tries, but keep on looking.

Whatever the quality of the relationship with a manager or agent, however, do not let him do all the work and then, when things don't go well, cry and scream and fire him and hire someone new to blame. You must know what you want and take some responsibility for getting it. No manager or agent will ever be 100 percent reliable and helpful. The best he can do is to make connections and deals for you. And if what you want is superstardom, don't lie to yourself. You may have to be willing to get involved in a bit of a Faustian exchange to hit the big time, so don't pretend you want to stay pure as Mozart if you want an Oscar.

Along with a demo, the composer/performer may also be asked to submit a video to record companies' prospective managers or concert promoters. And should a manager express interest in you, make sure it is the music that is being sold and not you. It can be seductive to be told that you will be marketed as an actor or a personality, but it is not good for your music.

A composer/performer shouldn't waste time waiting for the response of record companies. An active musical life yields more technical facility, and personal experience is grist for the creative mill. You should try to play clubs and festivals no matter how small, because pop, rock, and country music depends on a dialogue with its audience. Audience response provides a valuable energy to test the accessibility of your material as well as the vitality of your performance. When you perform your own beloved songs for audiences who are talking, eating, or restless, you find out how to sharpen your concentration, and you learn what focuses attention in a room. Later, when you go back to your writing, you understand which music wins over crowds and which ought to be played for audiences predisposed to new music. You also begin to discover how much audience

approval matters to you. A fine composer/performer like
Bruce Springsteen develops his material so that he and the
audience are involved in a give-and-take as intense as a
revival meeting. I can't imagine his music without the added
element of impassioned mass cheers and sing-alongs. Bob
Dylan or Tom Waits, on the other hand, often write more
interestingly when not aiming to please; for example, Dylan
was booed off the stage at the Newport Folk Festival when
he tried to move his sound into the electric age.

As composer/performer, you needn't define yourself by
good or bad experiences on the stage, but early in your
career, live performances can teach you not only your
strengths and weaknesses but also about timing, amplifica-
tion, lengths of sets, and order and interpretation of songs. I
opened several times for Dave Van Ronk at the Café Lena
in Saratoga Springs and was fascinated by his gritty interpretations of Brecht and his use of the open-tuned steel folk
guitar with Kurt Weill's music. I listened as he juxtaposed a
funky jug band version of "Mack the Knife" against a raspy,
tender interpretation of Joni Mitchell's "Clouds." Later on
I remembered Van Ronk's style when I set Brecht's *Good
Woman of Setzuan* to music. I also remembered how much
the audience loved him, while they barely listened to me.
Working at Lena's taught me to write more simply and
dramatically and to balance introspective ballads with humor
and unexpected changes of pace. I never made any money
and I usually drove back to college feeling dreadful, but Van
Ronk used to say he thought I had something, and Lena
(who is still a great entrepreneur of young talent) said she
thought I might do better to write for the theater.

If, when you reach your late twenties, you are still
waiting on tables to earn a living, and your parents are
glaring at you whenever you see them, and you worry that
there are only three rock stars who have ever launched a
career when they were past thirty-five, and you wake up at

night sweating, then it's up to you to decide what you want to do. That you haven't made it doesn't mean that you are without talent. It doesn't mean that you don't have vision. It simply means that it is cruel and cold out there in the commercial world. And if you decide that you cannot keep going, you will not be judged. No one is writing a movie of your life.

Whatever you decide to do, the important thing is not to become bitter and angry and lie to yourself. There are many ways to do so. It's easy to blame the world and complain about people less talented than you who have achieved success and ignore the fact that you are not the only talented person ever to have gone undiscovered. You can tell yourself that the big break will come next week, that people will embrace you, that you're sure one break will lead to another. By doing this, you set yourself up time and again for disappointment. You can accuse someone of stealing your sound or your song and focus on this as the reason for your lack of success, whereas, as often happens, someone probably came up with the same idea at the same time you did. I have in my drawer right now a Pied Piper musical because there are three others in the works this year. I spent roughly half a day fulminating about the theft of my idea, but then I had to recognize that perhaps Robert Browning had more to do with the interest in this subject than I did. You can tell yourself that you work harder than anybody else, but you probably don't. You can say that nobody cares about good music, but there are people who do. When the lies and rationalizations become more important to you than the music itself, when you can't concentrate on your sounds and let them refresh you, then it's time to take a break.

Jazz is a particularly difficult field in which to survive. It is not mainstream music, and is even more marginal when it's experimental. Nobody who writes jazz really expects to have a hit. I've never known any jazz artist who had any familiarity with, or interest in, the notion of the hard sell. Jazz is a private discussion, in a unique language, between players and audiences, and to lose that quality would be to lose the essence of the music. Anyone contemplating a career as a jazz composer knows that and most likely accepts it.

The most perilous trap for a jazz artist to avoid is the martyrdom mentality. Just as some modern classical composers have their noses pointed toward the ceiling, so some people who write jazz have their chins pointed to their chests, luxuriating in the delicious self-righteousness to which their musical lot condemns them. This is dangerous indulgence and also a self-fulfilling prophecy. It closes off a whole innocent part of the public who is willing to listen to music for the sake of sounds, bravado, and poetry.

The most lucrative ways for jazz composer/performers to sustain themselves financially are to play their chosen instruments in pit orchestras for musical theater, at gigs for parties celebrating bar mitzvahs, weddings, and so on, and in recording sessions. Session work is lucrative, quick, and relatively painless, but the danger is in becoming hooked on the lucrative fees for those who play this consumer music, just as it is for the people who write it. Breaking into the difficult, high-powered world of contractors and commercial producers can seem like quite a coup. Also, busy schedules are great excuses for not writing. I know three saxophonists who make lots of money and do nothing but lament about how little time they have for their own music. The truth is, they're addicted to security. If you spend too much time playing jingles or music for certain kinds of movies, or take too many weddings or bar mitzvahs, your listening powers can be dulled by the music's repetitive quality and lack of depth. The rote nature of the work fatigues the ear, and you stop listening to the reverberation of sounds for overtones; the strength and freshness of your hearing diminish. So be careful, if you decide to do this kind of work, that you don't do too much of it. A young composer must maintain a balance between what her life requires and what her music demands. The business side of music is peopled by those who "just took this job for a while," and have stayed there, addicted to its comforts and security. Satisfying one's basic need is one thing, but copping out is another—though it often goes under the name of disillusionment, maturity, practicality, and so forth. A young composer must be willing to take risks and sacrifice everyday comforts for the struggle in which her vocation will be tempered and proved.

EIGHT

Writing as a Woman

On a recent plane trip from Boston to New York, I sat next to a woman who said she was a conductor. I said I was a composer. It was a stunning moment for us both, one we had never experienced before, one we would be unlikely to experience again. The odds against two such rare birds meeting in this way would have to be astronomical. Although plane rides are troublesome for me, I barely noticed this one, so absorbed was I in our conversation, which reminded me yet again of how far behind women are in the composing and conducting fields.

In the musical arena, women have historically been considered, and accepted, as performers. Divas have always been the objects of tribute, even worship. Great women instrumentalists have been warmly acknowledged (though it has been an unwritten rule until quite recently that instruments such as the saxophone, trumpet, tuba, and bass were off-limits to female players). Pop and rock singers have achieved fame and fortune commensurate with their male peers in the field. It has been taken for granted that women have talent in these areas, that they can be artists in their own right. But try to lead a rock and roll rhythm section of all males. The gender differences are as palpable as they would be if you tried to quarterback a football team.

For those women who have sought to work in capacities in which they exert maximum control, the journey has been an even more rugged one. You need only the fingers of one hand to count the women composers who have had musicals produced on Broadway. Ellen Taaffe Zwilich recently won the Pulitzer Prize for music, but it was the first time that had ever happened. Scores for major feature films, films with the highest budgets and the biggest stars, are rarely written by women. No woman is the principal conductor of any major symphony orchestra in this country, though women occasionally make guest-conducting appearances.

With regard to composing, I think one reason why it lags so far behind other fields in its opportunities for women is that it is essentially a behind-the-scenes endeavor. From a historical point of view, we know that Clara Schumann used her husband's name to get her works performed. Fanny Mendelssohn published under the name of her brother Felix. The nineteenth-century audience was unwilling to accept the notion of a woman's musical intellect. Modern audiences may be ready for a woman's music, but certainly the male-dominated inner sanctum of conductors, musical directors, and producers is not. Musical politics, by its nature, is not something that people see. It happens off-camera. And because of that, there is no pressure for men to behave in a "liberated" fashion for appearance' sake.

It became unconscionable, in recent years, for women to be excluded from medicine and literature, from political office, from the astronaut corps. These are visible positions of power and/or prestige, and the absence of women from them eventually became glaring. No such pressure exists in the world of musical composition to force men to share power with women. Composers, for the most part, stay behind the scenes. When an activity is not visible, such change is bound to happen more slowly.

And it is not a simple issue that can be explained by citing men's intransigence. Blaming men for the present state of affairs is neither helpful nor completely truthful.

The weight of history itself has kept conditions the way they are today. From the most superficial perspective, a woman may sit at a harpsichord but not wield a baton because the former is feminine and the latter is phallic. Neither she nor an audience can easily accept the vigorous, commanding stature, the aggressive commands, of the arm and baton. In the past, a woman was unlikely to stay up all night writing a symphony because there was no precedent for a woman having control over a hundred instruments playing fast, loud, and hard. Similarly, a woman would be far less likely to hammer out tunes for a Broadway musical in the thirties and forties because the music involved emotional textures— bawdy, furious, raucous, desperate, mocking, and so forth— that were not thought to be proper, ladylike ones. It took a man to write "You Can't Let a Man Walk All Over You" for a singer/actress. The distance between the writer and the performer restored the sense of propriety. In other words, women could publicly express vindictive feeling as long as men gave them the words and music. It is important to understand that the musical voice comes from a place deep in the unconscious and as such is an extremely powerful one. It evokes a response that goes far beyond the social conventions and touches the potent emotions of sexual desire, of primal need and fear. In many cultures, it has seemed unlikely for women to want to be potent enough to exercise these powers. And those who did would be able to terrify and intimidate the group. Such fears, grounded in long-standing sexist mythology, obviously are difficult to dispel.

Though there has been progress, woman composers are still greatly ignored in theatrical, classical, and jazz idioms. San Francisco boasts a women's chamber orchestra, Los Angeles a female big band orchestra called Maiden Voyage. Holly Near has founded Red Wood Records, a label devoted to women's music. And generally women are breaking through in the areas of opera and experimental performance by producing and conducting their own works. I'm not one to wait around for a male music director to choose my ballet or chamber piece for performance. I do what I can to initiate performances even if they have a budget one-eighth as large as a funded institutional production. I know I have to be aggressive and that, at times, I threaten my male peers. I don't like feeling harsh and being the object of condescension and mockery. I want to work with men and share music with them because music is a mirror of our chemistry, moods, attractions, repulsions, and mutual discomfort— such feelings feed the compositional fire. But a portion of almost every day of my working life is also devoted to some struggle with sexism, and every woman composer I know has to cope with anxiety and depression because the jobs and funding, already so scarce, are almost unavailable to them.

So what survival tactics can women use in a situation that can only be described as hellish? If I go to a recording studio for a session with thirty musicians for a film score I've written, I make sure I look good and behave professionally, and if one musician tries to undermine me, I make clear that I know what I'm doing and what I expect from him or her. I try to do so with quiet authority and dignity. If straight-forwardness and calmness fail me, I have a look I inherited from my mother that could freeze an army. Another strategy is silence, which can sometimes bring rowdy musicians to their senses. The most important weapon of all is a stinging wit.

Women cannot afford the luxury of sulking over insults. A bleeding heart will get you nowhere. We must, when we suffer a reverse, pick ourselves up and keep going (we tend, I think, to recover more quickly than men, and though this may not be all to the good, the situation demands it: a man may take a year to recover from being savaged by the *New*

York Times; a woman, of necessity, snaps back sooner). No one is interested in complaints. As revolutionary political movements remind their followers, complaining doesn't do any good, it doesn't change anything. So get up, brush yourself off, buy a new dress (borrow the money if you have to), get the latest eye shadow, check to make sure that you have your favorite pen, your tape deck has batteries, and start over.

It is important for you to feel that you are a lady, whatever sort of lady you wish to be. Don't be cornered into playing a role. Don't cultivate a grubby, dour, workaholic image because you think that is what is appropriate for a female composer. You can read *Cosmopolitan,* or *The New Yorker,* or the *New York Review of Books* and still write wonderful symphonies. Make some kind of life for yourself outside of music, whether it focuses on friendships, downhill skiing and hiking, or cooking pasta. This will help to sustain you in periods of musical drought. Develop a sense of humor, even if the best you can do is a pained Eastern European smirk.

Recognize that it is not fruitful to push beyond what can be realistically accomplished. This does not mean that you shouldn't be aggressive in pursuing your goals. Instead of outright hostility, you will more often confront the passive kind from male agents, managers, and other powers that be who will be less willing and prompt to do things for women than they are for men, less apt to follow up and really push you forward. This kind of resistance to helping is often unintentional and subconscious, and if you can recognize that you will be less likely to sink into bitterness. Learn how to promote yourself. When someone promises to call and doesn't, you call him. When someone promises to show you a performance space and doesn't, go to the space yourself and use his name. In other words, take responsibility for making things happen.

Keep track of everything you record, everything you write, and keep sending things out, and sending things out, and sending things out. (This applies to male composers as well, of course, but in this, as in everything, women must be even more diligent and dogged.) Be in touch with women's organizations that are involved in music and work with them, though not to the exclusion of other groups. If you become known as a "women's composer," you'll be met by the prejudice that makes people feel you don't have what it takes to write for most "professional" situations. At the same time, don't abandon your fellow females, as women are apt to do in the theater, for instance, the moment they get a nod from a male producer or theater owner. Should you find yourself in a position of power, use it to secure work for other women. This is the way to make and solidify changes.

Success came to me early, and because of that, I didn't recognize that the difficulties of a composer's life, especially a female composer's life, are truly formidable. I can remember, when I was twenty-four or -five, sitting in on a meeting at Marlo Thomas' house and listening to a group of formidable women plan a network TV special celebrating the women's movement. As these songwriters, composers, screenwriters, producers, directors, and performers spoke of their last ten years and the prejudice and hardship they'd coped with, I felt mostly curious. When I stated my position, the women were surprisingly tolerant. They didn't exactly say "You'll learn," but rather expressed the hope that my experience meant that things would be better for my generation. My understanding changed over the next years, and the revelations were painful. When I ceased being the darling composer and musical director for the male-dominated experimental theater and began to write for myself instead, my popularity diminished. Every measure I wrote was no longer brilliant. My own pieces were not immediately accepted by theaters, as they had been when

I'd collaborated with males. When I was old enough to be considered a woman, I ceased being an unthreatening child to be discovered, taught, and protected. My mistakes weren't dealt with by paternalistic lectures and vows of paternal loyalty. A weak scene in a show wasn't a temporary problem, but proved I was a potential liability. Bad reviews threatened my funding; nasty reviewers treated me like a stupid, naughty girl. My budgets weren't considered responsible, and when I fought back for ideals and forms that came from deep within my musical soul, I was labeled hysterical or neurotic. The stronger I fought for myself, the more self-involved and unreliable I seemed. What would be called adventurous for a man was careless for me; prolific for a man was facile for me; opinionated, passionate, strong for a man was schoolmarmish, hectoring, strident for me. Unbeknownst to me, I had entered a dangerous sexual combat zone, full of power struggles, critical prejudice, and political games. When the reality changed, my awakening was extremely rude. Unprepared, I ricocheted from devastation to rage to false flirtation, subservience, and rebellion until finally I learned to stop reacting, rebuild my confidence, and fight for the life of my music. It might have been saner and healthier to give up under this stress, and I've wanted to, but a composer has little to turn to in the "real world." What else would I do with the sounds in my head? I'm reconciled now to being a female composer. But I would have been better equipped to face hardship and disappointment if I had had, from the outset, a more realistic view of my profession.

NINE

Success, and Then What?

BY NOW I HAVE MADE IT CLEAR that the chances of achieving success as a composer are slim. But occasionally it happens, and when, for whatever mysterious reasons that govern such matters, a composer's talent is recognized, he or she must then confront the issue of surviving success, which has its own hazards. Financial rewards usually accompany fame and recognition, and after years of economic drought, they come as an enormous relief. Celebrity itself, which the composer has probably consistently debunked, is heady. And the composer, rather like a neglected child suddenly showered with affection, cannot conceive of going back to the condition of needing and not having, of being neglected, unappreciated, unsupported, isolated, sometimes insulted. Perhaps a conductor has taken you up and begun to champion your music, or an executive person at a record company is an enthusiastic supporter, or a producer wants to do not only your current musical, but also your next one. Of course this is a dream come true. It also seems imperative to sustain such interest. How unbearable it would be to give up the conductor, the executive, the producer, and return to anonymity and wretchedness. So the dilemma becomes this: do you keep exploring and creating the risks that help you to look for original sounds and fresh motivations, or do you repeat the music that brought you the fame and acceptance in the first place? Unfortunately, the latter is the more common choice.

It is helpful, I think, to operate on the premise that most success is an accident, an extraordinary conjunction of events that happens rarely. How often does the composer have an exquisite aural vision and manage to get exactly the sounds he or she wants on paper and in performance, and then have critics and audiences listen to the music, understand the intent, and, on top of all that, like it? The answer is obvious. So it is dangerous, when this does happen, to consider it a preview of what lies ahead. And it isn't helpful to model your timetable after a biography of a prematurely successful talent. It is more likely that early in your career you will experience failure. And it is better if you do, for nothing will be more valuable to you than your own failures and their lessons.

It is important first of all to learn to take responsibility for your mistakes. Don't wallow in them and write off your whole career, but try to extract specific information about your weaknesses. Let's say you have seen a deer crossing a rocky field, which is lit by amber autumnal light, and the whole scene makes you hear a timpani, a flute—an alto flute—and some sustained notes on a couple of violins and cellos and a pad of Yamaha Dx7 horns. You find, however, when you put in the timpani, that the music sounds like a parody of the score for a scene in a bad Western in which the Indians come riding over the hill bent upon a massacre. You learn from this that you don't know much about timpani. Well, that's not the end of the world. That can be corrected. Don't look for justifications for your lack of knowledge. They are always available, but lying to yourself leads to creative death.

Be willing to admit larger failures as well. I once wrote a musical called *Lullabye and Goodnight,* the one about a pimp and a hooker I mentioned earlier. I made her a member of the prostitutes' union, who organizes his stable and turns them against him, even as she is falling in love with him and he with her. It failed dismally and publicly. It failed the people who sang in it, who were faithful friends and worked very hard. It failed the producer, who had a lot of money in it. And of course it failed me.

The mistake I made was to concentrate on the music at the book's expense. I wrote one of my best scores, one that reflected all the violence and sensuality inherent in the story. The lyrics, derived from both the Bible and from street language, were strong. I thought that the book was relatively unimportant, that it would somehow find itself, that I didn't need to make concessions to it, and that if rewriting were necessary, I could do it in ways that brought the strongest music forward. I was wrong; the show bombed.

My first response was to retreat and lick my wounds and think a lot about how I had lost my talent, an understandable but rather useless reaction. The constructive use of the failure came when I was able to admit to myself: you have a problem with the book; you're more interested in what you can do musically, how you can use sounds to evoke dramatic imagery, than you are in the arc of a plot; so you had better either collaborate with a book writer or adapt a story. I plan to do *Lullabye and Goodnight* next year with an entirely new book.

This experience freed me and taught me to understand that the best music in theater comes from the organic movement of the story; the visual reality grows, the story becomes complex and intense, the characters develop, the themes arise naturally, and the music reflects the progress of all these elements working together. But only through a gross failure would I have understood my own weakness. Often the very pieces that have been successful for us, internally and externally, are the ones that trap us and make us unable to move out of the ruts they have created. A juicy failure, a good rap on the head, often contains the seeds of new understanding whose fruit is freedom.

Failure can also put you in touch with the strength of your commitment to your art. Let's say you have been declared an incompetent composer by every newspaper in New York and Washington. I've been in that position, and it's certainly not a comfortable one. It can interfere with sleeping, eating, living, even breathing. But if you don't fold in the face of this, if you continue to work, you will learn just how necessary your music is to you, how much you are willing to bear in pursuit of it.

Of course, the fact remains that failure is extremely painful, and I don't mean to advocate it for its own sake. However, a generation saturated by the messages of *Fame*, *Flashdance*, and *Dirty Dancing* tends to have an unrealistic sense of the time it takes to achieve success and what the term "success" means. Today's young composers are impressed by the final result of a working process and less able to benefit from the subtle lessons learned from committing oneself to a day-to-day, one-step-forward-one-half-step-back process of labor. Life's experiences are rendered by the mass media as being mostly black and white, and therefore failure can't be seen as a part of the process, but only as a disaster in itself. Because you live in an era deeply influenced by media-style reactions and because you are in a profession that is inherently intense and dramatic, your failures may seem to happen on a grand scale. But they are no more excruciating than the disappointments endured by human beings who lead less histrionic lives. So do not exalt your pain and use it as an excuse to play the tragic victim.

Also, do not con yourself into buying the myth that the closer you are to the edge, the richer, more significant, more interesting, more urgent your work will be. This school of behavior, which thrived in the sixties and continues to a somewhat lesser degree today, is based on a romance with danger and debauchery, and generally is sustained by heavy drug use. Work produced while you are in the grip of this myth will be born of a youthful, falsely motivated energy, and however compelling it is, it will not be the best work of which you are capable. I've lost many friends to this myth, and when I listen to their music now, I wonder what they might be writing if they had the courage to live through the fantasy, to cut out their self-destructiveness even if it meant losing their power for a time. Eventually they would likely have found a new voice reflecting their experiences and capable of imagining more deeply. Jazz and rock composers are known for "selling their souls" to cut one album or get a club date. The desperation to rise rapidly to the top in a youth-oriented business causes a lack of perspective. They cannot see themselves composing or playing at forty-five. But the public is changing, and, in any case, there's no knowing what one might write at sixty.

Classical composers can shut out the world by becoming snobbish and paranoid. They close off from their friends and audiences by becoming increasingly bitter. They self-destruct by refusing to find jobs, living off friends and/or wives, and ultimately their defensiveness cuts them off from a possible community of peers. Rock and roll seems to breed the exhibitionist who falls in flames at the peak of his career. Classical composers more often fade away into increasing alienation, poverty, bad music, obscurity. At this stage of my life, I find both scenarios childish, and though my heart breaks for the friends I see who are helplessly in love with their self-destructive tendencies, I know that I live in an age in which too many people are suffering and dying through no fault of their own, which makes me impatient with those who play with their lives.

Longevity is difficult to achieve in a society intent upon using up its artists in a very short time. Americans love to decree success quickly and, just as quickly, to snatch it away. In order to withstand this, you must have faith in yourself and take satisfaction from the changes and growth that occur in your creative powers. For time has gifts it bestows on the composer that can come from no other source.

Over time, your knowledge of the voices and instruments that are your tools of expression becomes much more subtle. Your knowledge of the harmonies and rhythms that best represent the world you want to create with your sounds becomes broader and more complex. It is like learning a language: the longer you speak it, the more fluent you become. Your knowledge of the subject matter available to you grows in direct proportion to your length of time on this earth: the more you hear and experience, the greater are the possibilities of things you want to address musically.

Randy Newman is a good example of a pop writer who has grown with time. At the outset of his career, his tone was primarily sardonic and he depended a great deal on words. But over the years, his music has deepened melodically, his arrangements have become more provocative, he has explored video in an interesting fashion, and he has grown into writing film scores as well as songs. He has not sought the quick, splashy success that is based on cultivating an image; he has instead concentrated on his music and steadily moved forward.

In my own case, each year that passes makes me more aware of my limitations in the past. I am just about to begin writing my first classical opera, a form for which I used to have an avid distaste. When I thought of opera, I thought of people with big chests singing overblown music and walking around onstage like Japanese robots and falling and gasping and dying and having absolutely nothing to do with anything real or meaningful, and my reactions to all this ranged from scorn to abhorrence. I still respond this way to banal productions of the old war-horses that make up such a large part of most opera companies' repertoires. But I have come to see, with time, that the operatic form represents the height of theatricality, and far from being arid and stale, it is dynamic and spirited. It has everything: music, theater, dance, visual art. It is the banana split of musical forms. But if you had told me ten years ago that I would think that today, I would have collapsed in laughter.

As a young composer, try to recognize how little you still know about your own sounds and about the world around you. Continuous study is helpful and humbling in this regard. It forces you to see all the things that exist that you haven't begun to touch. This is why you should experiment with forms that lie far afield from your area of focus. Try your hand at a percussion concerto, or a song cycle. Write a scene for an opera. You needn't even show it to anyone. The point is to keep yourself open to a variety of musical experiences, to try to understand why certain forms exist, to avoid negating music that differs from your own. There are in the world a multitude of places to go to, literally and metaphorically, and just as many things to care about and be hungry for.

It seems to me from my present vantage point that there are two stages to a composer's life (perhaps there are more that I have yet to experience). The first is madly prolific and fiery and narcissistic and filled with a sense of a discovery of one's own sounds. The world, so amazing and full, if rather feverish, is quite small because it is limited to what you know, and you haven't lived long enough to know very much. The second stage, which I haven't inhabited very long, is also marked by a passion to reach people through sound, but it encompasses as well the realization that you and the world are separate, that you are simply one member of the human race, that other people and places undreamed of exist, and that these can in time be brought into your work to enrich it.

There are people who embark on a composing career seeking the kind of fame and prestige that is measured by receiving a Pulitzer or a Grammy or high sales on the charts or seeing your picture on the cover of *Time* magazine. There are some who want to be recorded or played by the best orchestras, or conducted by the most well-known conductors. But it is likely that as they mature they will come to terms with the fact that composing is not a superstar profession, that it is unlikely to fulfill such fantasies, and that they will never, in fact, receive the kind of praise and adoration lavished on a glitzy, sequined rock and roller or a barrel-chested, relentlessly charming tenor.

Listeners immediately take music to their heart and assume ownership of it. In that moment of appropriation, the composer is, in a sense, obliterated, wiped out. Music, as opposed to poetry or tap dancing or acting or any other artistic form you can name, is like a force of nature. It is, as I have said, a visceral event, a sensual one. You can feel its vibrations in your body. And when you do, the least important thing in the world is the person who patched it together, the one who directed that this note be put here, that one there, that the line move up or down, that it last or get cut off, that a space exist, or a da-da-da-da sound in the bass line.

This invisibility, I should add, is desirable, even though it may not gratify certain of the composer's fantasies. I had to learn this for myself at no small price. My early career was uncharacteristically public, and I developed a persona that was all too visible. I also talked, for the record, a great deal about my music—why I used bird sounds, strange languages, or ethnic instruments—and eventually all this got in the way of my simply doing it. Only by shedding the persona was I really able to concentrate on the music. Another drawback to being a "personality composer" is that the audience listens to your music with your commentary in mind, your newspaper photos, your bio. And no real composer wants that. A real composer wants his or her music to have multilevels of definition and form of its own for the listener.

So what expectations should a young composer have about recognition? Is it realistic to have any at all? Perhaps the only sound one is that you be reckoned with by your peers. Your music should be bright enough and strong enough and identifiable enough to make a significant statement, so that when a list of interesting composers is proffered, you're on it. This does not mean that you will be honored. You may, in fact, be reviled. That is a reckoning. You have been paid attention to. You exist.

As for praise, I've indicated the capriciousness you can expect the world at large. And from your colleagues, your co-workers, it will most likely be tepid, if it comes at all: "That was almost interesting" . . . "I think it'll work." Do not wait for "gorgeous," "beautiful," "fantastic." I have heard much more criticism than I have praise from people I have worked with over the years, and it took me a long time to recognize that they liked my work or they wouldn't be doing it. Their acknowledgment of me, their regard for my talent, was inherent in their performing my music, not just once but over and over again.

Perspective is something one can only develop with time, though it is an important resource for surviving as a composer. You'll come to see that the pain you suffer when your sounds don't come together right is a bit ridiculous when it is set beside other pain-producing circumstances that exist in the world. Being an artist is a privilege; you should become tough enough to pay the price willingly for that privilege. Your primary reality and reward should be the world of your sounds. If you write for acceptance, understanding, applause, or liberation, you will be disappointed. If you write for your own artistic, intellectual, and sensual pleasure, you will be fine. At the same time, don't neglect the moral dimension that your work may have. This does not mean that you must become a noble creature living on a lofty plane. It simply means that you believe that part of the composer's job is to wake up people and remind them of such things as dignity and compassion and beauty, which they have been neglecting.

When a commission is dangled before you, or a producer wants to see the first draft of a musical, or an orchestra is rumored to be considering doing an evening of your work, allow yourself to take some pleasure in the possibility but don't become obsessed with the outcome. Don't bore your friends with endless talk about it; don't wait by the phone like a hopeful high school sweetheart. These reactions will simply sap the energy you need to keep writing, sending things out, and exploring new sounds. You can't afford to put your life on hold while you wait to see if some tantalizing prospect comes to fruition. The commission may fall through, the producer may go bankrupt, the orchestra may decide to go with Beethoven. But the grant application you submit, the tape you get to a record company, or the new music you write may be the very things that pay off six months or a year from now.

In order to strike a balance between elation and despair, it is important to know that some conductor or producer saying he or she likes a piece of work has very little to do with whether or not the work will be done. Particularly in this culture, at this time, there is an abundance of cowardice on the part of those people who are in positions to say yes or no to composers. More often than not, they prefer to say maybe and then ignore you, rather than to say no and tell you why. So if someone indicates something may happen, tell a friend or two, let them share your momentary pride and briefly act as cheerleaders, because composing is isolated and scary work and you need that kind of sustenance now and then. But do not stop what you are doing now, because chances are greater than not that the job will vanish into the vapor.

I used to approach everything negatively: "This will never happen" . . . "They won't want it" . . . "I'm sure I'll be turned down." While that protected me from the pitfalls of high expectations, it also robbed me of the pleasure I was entitled to feel at having come as far as I had. You can afford to feel good about being wanted, about having people interested in you; at the same time, recognize that many obstacles will arise between the time when a project is in the planning stage and its completion.

We live in a world that is saturated with sound, much of it music. It washes over us in supermarkets, doctors' offices, department stores. We channel it into our own ears as we walk down the street. It is there on the other end of the phone while we wait to be connected with someone. It comes at us from television sets, video recorders, records, tapes, discs. In many instances, we have no choice in the matter. We are bombarded by it whether we like it or not. The British musician Constant Lambert complained that we lived in an age of "tonal debauch" . . . and that decadence has increased to staggering proportions.

The perpetual stream of sound that floods our senses is numbing. Also, we come to take music for granted. Stravinsky, who deplored such easy access to music, wished that people would have to *walk* to concerts in order to hear his music. He believed their willingness to do so would indicate a true desire to hear the music, and once there, they would fully appreciate it.

Though records, tapes, and discs supply fantasy to the solitary listener, they take the listener for granted and the listener returns the favor. In a concert, performers, audience, and music are alive; they affect one another. But today, hearing music in concert is the exception rather than the rule. Our ears don't have to work for the sounds they want to hear. They are available at the push of a button. And just as unworked muscles grow slack and flaccid, our ears become lazy. Our listening energy loses focus until eventually we are unable to discover the remarkable fine details of music—the overtones, subtle crescendos, dialogues, and fundamental themes from the heart. It is hard to know whether music begins to sound the same because it is carelessly written or whether our listening has become undisciplined and undiscerning.

More often than not today, music is treated as merchandise, and, as such, it is subject to the same principles that guide the marketing of other products. Label recognition is a key factor in achieving any sort of popularity. A young composer whose music falls into a recognizable category— soft rock, fusion jazz, nostalgic jazz, minimalism, innovative musical theater, New Wave punk, etc.—will most likely do better than the composer who writes music that cannot be pigeonholed stylistically. In theory, anything goes today musically, but there is so much of everything that it is hard to achieve an identity without being dumped into a category. People who refuse to let this happen to them are generally described as "eclectic," or not described at all because they disappear very swiftly.

In the din of this noisy marketplace, how is a young composer to develop a singular musical voice and get it heard? The only voice that ever rises above the racket is a true one, a voice shaped by a pure motivation. A pure motivation is simple and fresh, and comes out of the composer's childlike discovery of the world as a painting with sound. Perhaps the impulse behind a particular piece of music is love for another person, as it often is for a poet writing a sonnet. Or perhaps the music is a eulogy, triggered by a deep sense of loss or grief. Or the celebration of a stirring event. Or perhaps it is simply a sound: the whisper of a flute, a voice from another room, a car driving over a snowy street. Whatever generates it, a pure motive is like a splash of cold spring water on the composer's face, awakening in him or her the desire to build a structure that reflects this fresh outlook toward sounds and the instruments that make them. The feeling of discovery—that this moment has never happened before—combines with the composer's practical knowledge and dexterity of technique, and a true musical voice emerges. When this happens, it is an occasion for celebration. It means that the world's ears, exhausted though they may be by constant exposure to homogenized sounds, can still hear something that is true and respond from the heart.

I don't think that a well-meaning individual who gets dressed and puts on a hat and coat and travels by cab, car, or subway to the concert hall or theater wants simply to submit to an entertainment that offers distraction and/or anesthesia. I think, rather, that he or she wants to be awakened and told something about the inner world, about dreams, about an existence that transcends the banality of life. When a piece of music, like any work of art, is good, it makes everything more intense: feelings of love and desolation, sexual feelings, the longing to travel, the desire to move freely, to taste real adventure, the wordless passing back and forth of knowledge between parent and child, the lust of wisdom and humor for seeing things in an unexpected way. I think it is the composer's job to carry the audience beyond the imprisoning daily world, to make them feel they are not alone, that there is another place we all inhabit. This is, in a sense, our culture's ritual, often unrecognizable because it is badly done, performed in the wrong place, by the wrong witch doctor, transmitting the wrong messages. But the impulse, the longing to be aroused and altered, continues. And on those occasions when it is satisfied, there is great cause for hope.

Always, for the composer, the primary joy of music is that she hears it. Whether you make it yourself on a keyboard or sing it with a guitar, get together an instrumental trio or singers to do a three-part harmony, assemble a chamber group, rock band, or jazz ensemble to play what you have composed—the point is that you can hear the music, and there is no greater reward than that. There is no substitute for the experience of being engulfed in your own music. I feel that my life, despite its ups and downs, has been remarkable and blessed because I have heard so much of my music, and it has been done so well. I've heard it inside and outside, in basements, in theaters, surrounded by stone walls, sung by old people and by children, played by wonderful players. Nothing can alter that or take that away from me.

Once you have had the experience of making a piece of music from a pure motivation, and the mechanics of execution are professional and sound, and the performance contains that perfect balance of dignity and vigor that is so exquisite, it is hard to be satisfied by less, to write music that is counterfeit or derivative or facile. Because when all the elements are right, there is another presence in the music, a spiritual presence. It needn't be God. It's hard to believe it isn't magic. It certainly is harmony. You heard sounds inside your head and now you are hearing them played back to you, and they represent what your notion of beauty is. That moment is extraordinary and inimitable and precious. And nothing else exists in it—not concerns about money, bookings, agents, rehearsal space, grants, audience reaction, reviews, or acceptance—but the music itself. If you are a real composer, you know absolutely that that is more than enough.

Index